UNIX and C

A Book on C
AL Kelley and IRA POHL.
— Benjamin/Cummings Publishes
#* Looks pretty good

UNIX™ and C

A tutorial introduction

PHILIP CORNES

Computer Centre
Staffordshire Polytechnic

CHAPMAN & HALL

University and Professional Division

London · Glasgow · Weinheim · New York · Tokyo · Melbourne · Madras

Published by Chapman & Hall, 2-6 Boundary Row, London SE1 8HN, UK

Chapman & Hall, 2-6 Boundary Row, London SE1 8HN, UK

Blackie Academic & Professional, Wester Cleddens Road, Bishopbriggs, Glasgow G64 2NZ, UK

Chapman & Hall GmbH, Pappelallee 3, 69469 Weinheim, Germany

Chapman & Hall Inc., One Penn Plaza, 41st Floor, NY 10119, USA

Chapman & Hall Japan, Thomson Publishing Japan, Hirakawacho Nemoto Building, 6F, 1-7-11 Hirakawa-cho, Chiyoda-ku, Tokyo 102, Japan

Chapman & Hall Australia, Thomas Nelson Australia, 102 Dodds Street, South Melbourne, Victoria 3205, Australia

Chapman & Hall India, R. Seshadri, 32 Second Main Road, CIT East, Madras 600 035, India

First edition 1989
Reprinted 1990, 1991, 1992, 1994

© 1989 Philip Cornes

Typeset in 10½/12pt September by Leaper and Gard Ltd, Bristol
Printed in Great Britain by St Edmundsbury Press Ltd, Bury St Edmunds, Suffolk

ISBN 0 412 38160 5

The publisher makes no representation, express or implied, with regard to the accuracy of the information contained in this book and cannot accept any legal responsibility or liability for any errors or omissions that may be made.

A catalogue record for this book is available from the British Library

Contents

Acknowledgements

I should like to thank all those who made input to this volume from Stafford-shire Polytechnic, and in particular Duncan Shortland for his time, advice and hardware support. I should also like especially to acknowledge the contribution of my wife Ruth for her patience, her understanding and her typing.

Phil Cornes, 1989

Preface

This book does not pretend to answer all possible questions on UNIX and C – that would just not be possible in a volume of this size. However, it does answer most of the questions that my students ask me, given that they have already been exposed to the basics of other programming languages and operating systems.

The book, then, is intended to be read by 'A' level and undergraduate students who already have some knowledge of the basics of programming and who need to learn about UNIX and/or C. The versions of UNIX and C actually covered in the book are the standard AT&T V.2 UNIX and the standard K&R C. However, the material is covered in such a way that it is applicable to all common variants of UNIX and their associated C compilers.

The style of the book itself is intended to be tutorial in nature rather than just being a reference book, though a comprehensive index is provided which will allow easy reference access to the topics covered.

The first six chapters of the book cover the major topics that students need to know about the UNIX operating system including: login, basic UNIX commands, the nature and structure of the UNIX file system, creating and editing files, important UNIX tools, the shell command processor and programming in a UNIX environment using the built-in shell programming language.

The next seven chapters cover the basic syntax and semantics of the majority of the C programming language. C is a language powerful and flexible enough to be used in all applications from stock control and invoicing to writing compilers and operating systems. Indeed, the vast majority of UNIX itself is written in C

Having treated UNIX and C as essentially two separate subjects, the last four chapters bring them both together again. Chapter 14 shows how C programs in a UNIX environment can call up UNIX commands, use the UNIX multitasking facilities and signal and communicate messages to each other in order to work together. Chapter 15 looks at using standard UNIX utilities to help create and maintain suites of C programs plus a section which addresses the special problems of debugging in C. Finally, Chapters 16 and 17 go through the development and implementation of a small compiler for a simple programming language. The implementation of the compiler is in two parts: the first part is written as a C program and the second part is written as a UNIX shell script, just to show how the two areas really can be made to work together.

Introduction

As you can see, this book is split into three parts. All the material was written with the subconscious intention that you should start at page 1 and work through in order until you reach the end. However, this idea is not cast in concrete, so if you have the particular desire to master C before shell scripts for example, then there is no reason why you should not skip to Chapter 7 straight after Chapters 1 and 4 (logging on and editing files). The only real restriction is that you will need to have read or be familiar with the material in Chapters 1 to 15 before you progress on to the last two chapters as they assume a working knowledge of the earlier topics. Where the input and output from UNIX command sequences are listed as examples, or sections of program listings are given in the text, then they are enclosed between pairs of horizontal lines to make them stand out. The parts that you need to type are in **bold** typeface and the responses are in ordinary print. When it is particularly important for you to see the original layout of some text presented by the system then a special typeface is used which was generated directly on a UNIX system. For example, the use of the **ps** command from Chapter 3.

```
$ ps
PID    TTY    TIME    CMD
827    011    0:17    sh
901    011    0:01    ps
```

This is only intended to demonstrate the layout of a command sequence – do not worry if it does not make any sense yet, it will by the end of Chapter 3.

PART ONE
The UNIX operating system

UNIX basics

1.1 LOGGING IN

In order to access a **UNIX** system, every user is allocated a login name. This should be supplied to you by your system administrator and in most installations your login name will uniquely identify you to the system.

The standard invitation to login to a UNIX system is given by the prompt:

login:

When you get the login prompt, you should enter your login name followed by pressing the return (or enter) key. Normally, the system will not process any of your input until you press return, so you should remember to do this at the end of each line that you type in.

In addition to a login name, your system administrator may also have allocated a password to you to make your login more secure and prevent unauthorized access to your programs and data files. If a password is required, then the system will prompt you with:

password:

You should now type in your password, again followed by return. You will find that the characters you type for your password are not echoed back to your terminal. The echo facility is temporarily disabled by the system while you enter your password, so that no one can look over your shoulder as you type and read your password from the screen. The character echo will be restored after you press return. If you make a mistake either in entering your login name or your password, the system will respond with the message:

login incorrect

and you will be invited to begin the login sequence again.

When you manage to login without error, the system will probably print out some kind of 'message of the day' with news or points of local system interest.

Finally, the system will print out a prompt. By default this is either a dollar symbol

$

or a per cent sign

%

and you are now ready to type in commands.

1.2 LOGGING OUT

It may seem strange to want to logout so soon after logging in, but now is a good time to find out how, along with sorting out how to stop a running program and how to edit command lines you are typing in. This will save you hurriedly trying to look them up when you really need to know.

To logout, then, all you need to do is to type the end-of-file (EOF) character. You will see what this means in more detail later, but for now all you need to know is that on standard UNIX systems the EOF character is ctrl–d ('control' and 'd' keys together). Some systems also allow either the command **exit** or **logout** to perform the same function. After logging on, pressing ctrl–d should return you to the login: prompt.

1.3 CORRECTING ERRORS

If you spot an error in the command line you are typing before you press return, then there are two possibilities. You can either go back along your command line with ERASE to delete characters one at a time, or you can use KILL which will delete the entire line so you can start again. Different UNIX systems represent erase and kill in different ways. The UNIX standards are to use the hash/pound (#) symbol for erase and the AT symbol (@) for kill.

For example, typing

$ **whom**

would be equivalent to typing

$ **who**

The system of using @ and # was fine when printing terminals were common, as you could see exactly what had been deleted. Now that VDU terminals are almost universally used, the characters typed for erase and kill have changed — the most common versions being either the backspace (ctrl–h) character for erase and the DEL (delete) key for kill, or the DEL key for erase and ctrl–u ('control' and 'u' keys pressed together) for kill. A simple test at the keyboard will easily establish the correct keys for your particular installation.

1.4 STOPPING A PROGRAM

Most of the commands and programs you run can be aborted by typing the

interrupt character for your installation, usually DEL or ctrl–c whichever
your system uses.

If you just want to pause a program that is producing lots of output to
your screen without aborting its execution, then this can be done with the
XOFF character which is ctrl–s. Listing output from the program can then be
resumed using the **XON** character which is ctrl–q.

To find out for sure what characters your system uses for the functions
interrupt, quit, erase and kill, type in the following command and read the
values from the top line of the resultant output (do not be surprised if most of
the rest of the information does not make too much sense just at the
moment):

$ **stty −a**
intr=DEL; quit= ˆ \; erase= ˆ h; kill=@; eof= ˆ d; eol= ˆ ‘

1.5 UNIX FILE SYSTEM

The UNIX file system is built up in an inverted tree structure of directories
and files. At the top of the structure is a directory called the root, which is
given the symbolic name **/**. Directories in general (including **/**) are just files
that contain information about other subdirectories and files. The root directory contains several subdirectories, some of which have names like **bin**,
etc, **lib** and **usr**. These subdirectories in turn contain information on
further files. For example, the **bin** directory contains a set of files that are the
binary executable programs for many day-to-day UNIX commands, **etc**
contains many more executable programs mainly used for system adminis-
trative purposes as well as several files of system data including the user's
password file! The directory **lib** is used to hold library files including the C
compiler and its libraries, and **usr** contains the user home directories as well
as directories of local user command programs.

Diagrammatically, this structure appears as in Fig. 1.1. Notice that Fig.
1.1 contains two directories labelled **bin**, one under the root directory (/)
and one under **usr**. This is quite acceptable as they both have different
parent directories. However, it does mean that some method needs to be
used to specify which of the two (or more) is required. This is done by specifying the full **PATH NAME** of the required file starting at the root. So **/bin**
is the full path name of the **bin** directory under root and **/usr/bin** is the full
path name for the **bin** directory under **/usr**. This process is repeated
through as many levels as necessary to get along the tree structure's branches
to the individual files at the leaves. This means that the system password file
is called **/etc/passwd** and Fred's home directory is **/usr/staff/fred**.

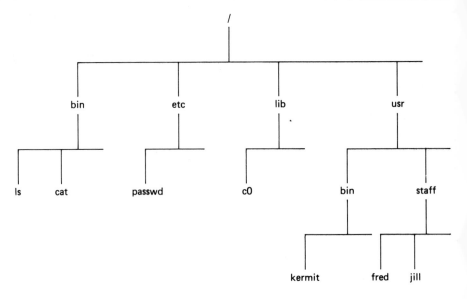

Fig. 1.1 Part of the UNIX directory structure.

1.6 WHAT IS IN A FILE?

Under UNIX a file is just a sequence of bytes (where each byte in a text file is large enough to hold a single character). The meaning of the data in a file depends entirely on the programs that use it — UNIX itself gives no meaning to the data, nor imposes any set order or structured layout on the file contents. This means that a program such as a text editor or compiler that is expecting a text file as input can easily be confused if a non-text file is supplied instead.

Simple UNIX commands | 2

Now you can logon, the next job is to look at some simple commands to get you started.

Type in the **who** command and the system will respond with something like the following:

$ **who**

```
you     tty02    Jul 16   14:17
pc      tty03    Jul 16   09:30
spt     tty12    Jul 16   10:24
mcw     tty21    Jul 16   12:34
djt     tty30    Jul 16   12:16
```

This is a list of all the users that are currently logged on to the system. The first column contains the list of login names of users logged on (and your login name will be one of them). The second column contains the terminal names at which the individual users are logged on. The last two columns contain the date and time of their current logon.

2.1 CONTACTING OTHER USERS

Now that you have a list of all the users on the system at this moment in time, you might like to chat to one of them via the terminal. This can be done with a command called **write** as follows:

$ **write name**

where name is the login name of the person you want to contact from column 1 of the **who** listing. The person you try to contact will then receive a message on their terminal of the form:

Message from you (ttyØ2)[Thu Jul 16 14:42]. . .

Anything you type now followed by RETURN will be sent to the receiver's terminal. To respond to your message, the person at the other end would just type:

$ **write you**

and anything that they type will then appear on your terminal.

When you have finished chatting, you can break the connection to each other by both sending the EOF character (ctrl–d you remember), and that will return you to the standard prompt with the system awaiting your next command. If you are doing something particularly urgent or demanding, it may be that you will not want to have your session interrupted to send or receive messages. In this case, all you need to do is to type:

$ mesg n

to ensure you will not be disturbed. To restore your terminal to its normally receptive state, you just type:

$ mesg y

and this will once again allow other users to write to your terminal with messages for you.

Sometimes it may happen that the person you want to contact is not currently logged on. In this case, what you want is to leave a message on the system that the other person can read next time they are on. This can be done with the command:

$ mail name

where **name** is the login name of the person to receive the message. Anything you type after this command up to an EOF character (ctrl–d) will be stored on the system waiting for the other person to logon.

Whenever you logon to the system, you can check to see if you have any mail (and read it if you have) just by typing:

$ mail

without any login name. The system will either report that you have:

No mail

or it will start to give you a listing of your messages. For example:

$ mail
From spt Thu Jul 16 15:24 GMT 1987
Hi Phil
Can I talk to you over lunch tomorrow at 12:3Ø
?

When you see the question mark prompt from **mail**, there are several options you can choose. Some are:

Press RETURN	**mail** goes on to the next message
Press —	**mail** returns to the previous message

Press d **mail** deletes the current message and then goes on to the next

Press q quit from **mail**

2.2 CHANGING PASSWORDS

If your login sequence does not require a password from you and you would like it to (you should), or you would like to change your existing password to something else, then this can be done with the following command sequence:

$ **passwd**
Changing password for you
Old password:

---

if you are changing an existing password, or:

$ **passwd**
Changing password for you
New password:

---

if you are supplying a new password for the first time. Either way, the system will eventually prompt you for a new password which will not be printed on your screen; so just to make sure that you typed what you thought you did, the system will then ask you to:

Re-enter new password:

which it will then check with your first attempt to make sure they match. You will now be required to use your new password each time you logon, so do not forget it or you will have to see the system administrator to get back into the system.

2.3 READING FILES

Normally, all the user passwords on a UNIX system are kept in a file called **/etc/passwd** which is usually open to be read by anyone on the system. The simplest way to do this is with the command:

$ **cat /etc/passwd**

Each line in this file is split up into seven parts (or fields) separated by colons and one line is associated with each person who has a login name on the system. A sample section of the listing might appear as follows:

```
you:64eAWhAYSK7aw:201:200:Your Name:/usr/you:/bin/sh
spt:XmhqVuUKWza..:287:200:S. Thomas:/usr/spt:/bin/sh
mot:JDz1bB9YZRXFw:291:200:M. Turner:/usr/mot:/bin/sh
jab:hMz51r91RD7QY:299:200:JA. Byrne:/usr/jab:/bin/sh
```

The first field (up to the first colon) is the user's login name — yours will also be listed. The second field is the user's password, but do not be surprised if, when you see yours, it does not make any sense. All the passwords have been encoded by the system for obvious security reasons. In fact, the method used to encode the passwords is so secure that it is considered quite safe to put the encoded versions on public view, so if you had sudden visions of trying to decode everyone's passwords, do not bother — it is not worth the effort! The third field is your user identity (uid) number on the system. It is just a numeric way of identifying you rather than using your login name. The UNIX system provides facilities set by the system administrator for allowing groups of users to work together on a project as a team, and the fourth field in **/etc/passwd** specifies the group identity (gid) number of the group of users that each login name belongs to. The fifth field is just a space for any comments, though it is usual to put the users' real names in this field and maybe their address or phone number as well. The sixth field specifies the directory path to each user's home directory. This is the directory that you will find yourself in by default straight after you have logged on. The last field is a command that will be executed for you automatically after logon. It is usually the name of a shell (**/bin/sh** for example) or it may be left blank, in which case it defaults to **/bin/sh** anyway.

The **cat** command (that you used to obtain the **/etc/passwd** listing) can be used to list the contents of any file, although if the file does not contain text then listing it to your terminal might cause some strange displays on the screen. The word 'cat' itself is an abbreviation of the word concatenate which means 'join together', and in fact as well as listing single files, **cat** can also be used to join files together before listing them. For example:

$ cat /etc/motd/ etc/passwd

will list your system's 'message of the day' file (**/etc/motd**) if it has one, followed immediately by the passwords file that you have already seen. One thing you will probably have noticed if your system has a fair number of users is that **cat** just lists all the way through a file without pauses, and that therefore you have to be a bit quick getting to the xoff (ctrl–s) character if you want to stop the listing from just scrolling off the screen. Unfortunately, there is no standard UNIX command that will cater for automatic pauses at the end of each page on a VDU, though most systems do provide a non-standard program to perform this task. On most systems this command is called **more**.

$ more /etc/passwd

should therefore provide the same listing as **cat** but without the rush to get to xoff. At each pause you press RETURN for the next line of the file, SPACE for the next page, or 'q' to quit the listing and return to the command prompt. If your system does not provide a **more** facility, do not worry, you will see how to provide your own version later as an example program.

Another useful command associated with text type files is called **wc**. This command is specifically useful where you want to know either a file's length in lines or in characters, or where you have a text file and want to know its word count. In fact, word counting is where **wc** gets it name from. For example:

```
$ wc /etc/passwd
42   6Ø   1993   /etc/passwd
```

From left to right the three numbers in the output are the number of lines in the file (42), the number of words in the file (60) and the number of characters in the file (1993). In the case of **/etc/passwd**, only the first and last numbers are useful. The first gives the number of login names on the system and the last is the file length in bytes. As **/etc/passwd** is not split up into words in the normal sense, the middle figure is meaningless in this case.

2.4 FILE SYSTEM MAINTENANCE

The next block of commands to look at are those needed to control your interaction with the file system. The first thing you want to know is how to find out where you are in the system directory structure. If you found your login name when you listed **/etc/passwd**, then the sixth field on your line gives the full path name through the directory structure to your home directory. This is the directory you should still be in (if you have not changed it) and you can check with a command that will print your current working directory:

```
$ pwd
/usr/you
```

Your actual result will differ from this, but the principles remain the same.

The next thing to do is to change directory and this can be done with the **cd** command:

```
$ cd /usr
$ pwd
/usr
$
```

Typing the first command above changes your current working directory to **/usr** and the **pwd** command following allows you to check that this is indeed the case. From anywhere in the directory structure typing just **cd** on its own will return you to your home directory. Try the following sequence:

```
$ cd
$ pwd
/usr/you
$
```

Sometimes it can be very tedious typing in a full path name for **cd** if, for example, you only want to move up a level in the directory structure to the parent directory of your current position. In this case, a special notation can be used to mean the parent of the current directory as follows:

```
$ cd ..
$ pwd
/usr
$
```

As you can see, the parent directory is indicated by the double full stops. If you need to go up more than one level in the structure you can:

```
$ cd ../../../..
```

would take you up four levels, for example. Typing **pwd** now will show just:

```
/
```

meaning that you have reached the top (or root) level of the directory. Typing too many double dots (as here) will not give you an error, but will not take you any higher than the root directory either.

Sometimes, you will need to refer to the current directory in a command when you may not know where you are. Again there is a special notation which in this case is just a single full stop. Try the sequence:

```
$ cd
$ cd ..
$ cd .
$ pwd
/usr
$
```

Make sure you understand the sequence, so that the result shown is what you expected.

Your current working directory is now the parent to your home directory, and it is likely that there will be many more users whose home directories are below this one. These can be listed with the command:

```
$ ls
```

djt	jur	mef	ps	you
dsh	ma	mot	spt	
jab	mcw	pc	tc	

The **ls** command can be used to list the contents of any directory you are allowed to see, just by specifying its name after the command. For example, to see the contents of your own home directory, type:

```
$ ls /usr/you
```

Unless you have already had something entered into your home directory, it will probably appear empty at this stage.

The **/usr/you** part of the command is called an absolute path name as it starts all the way up at the root directory (shown by the fact that the first character is a slash /). Path names can also be given relative to your current position in the directory structure. If you have been following the examples given so far, then your current directory is the parent of your home directory. The full relative path to your home directory from its parent directory is **./you**. (You remember that '.' means the current directory.) This can be further abbreviated just to **you** so that:

```
$ ls you
```

will give the same result as the previous command example.

On many systems, the security arrangements will be such that you will not be allowed to change directory into another user's home directory area. This means that if you try to change directory (**cd**) into one of the other directories listed in the current **ls** listing such as:

```
$ cd mot
```

you will probably get an error message to inform you that you are not allowed into this directory, such as:

```
$ cd mot
mot: bad directory
```

It would be useful if you could find out which directories you had permission to inspect without having to try them out one at a time. Indeed, it would also

be useful to find out which entries in a directory listing were themselves
subdirectories and which were ordinary files. This can be done by supplying
one extra parameter to the **ls** command:

$ ls −l /usr

The extra −l parameter tells the **ls** command to supply a long listing for all
the file information. Many UNIX commands can have extra parameters
supplied in this way and as a general rule the extra parameters directly follow
the command name and are preceded by a minus sign (−).

Typically, the long listing of a directory would appear as follows:

$ ls −l /usr/pc

```
-rwx------  1  pc      staff    21898  Jun 29  16:51  a.out
-rwxr-xr-x  1  pc      staff       44  Jul 21  10:08  back
drwxrwx--x  2  pc      staff      128  Jul 15  14:18  basic
-rw-------  1  pc      staff      193  Jun 29  16:51  ctest.c
drwx------  4  pc      staff       64  May 26   1986  lispdir
-rw-rw-r--  1  pc      staff     1656  Jun 23   1986  more.c
-rws--x--x  1  pc      staff    12027  Apr  2  12:29  zapem
```

A lot of new information is presented here, so let us work through it in
more detail. The leftmost column contains the access permissions for each
file in the listing. There are three sorts of ordinary user as far as a UNIX file is
concerned. First there is the actual owner of the file whose uid is given in
column 3 of the listing ('pc' in this case). Secondly, there is the group of users
that the owner belongs to with the gid in column 4 ('staff' in the example).
And finally there is everyone else on the system. Each of these three user
classes has an individual set of permissions to perform various operations on
a file. For an ordinary file, the basic operations are to read the file's contents,
to write new information to the file and to execute the file as a command
program. For a directory file these same operations become: read a file from
the directory, write a file to the directory and search through the directory
contents. Armed with this information, you can now interpret the meanings
of the file permission flags. The leftmost flag contains a letter d if the
associated file is a directory, or a dash (−) if it is an ordinary file. The next
three flags contain the read, write and execute (rwx) or read, write and
search (still rwx) permissions for the owner of the file. The next three flags
are the same access permissions for the file owner's group. The last three
flags are the permissions for everyone else on the system. From the sample
listing then, the line

```
-rwx------  1  pc      staff    21898  Jun 29  16:51  a.out
```

means that the file **a.out** is not a directory, that the owner (pc) can read,
write and execute the file, but that the group (staff) and everyone else cannot
access the file at all.

```
drwxrwx--x  2  pc        staff       128  Jul 15  14:18  basic
```

shows that basic is a directory, that the owner (pc) and all the members of group staff have read, write and search permissions on the directory, and that other users only have search permission. Because they do not have read and write access to the directory, other users cannot add or remove files from the directory. What they can do is to execute any files in the directory that have their own execute bit set for other users, or search other subdirectories that have their other users' x bit set, as long as they know the files exist and know their names.

The only file permissions in the example listing that you cannot yet understand are those for the file **zapem** and this is because of the letter s in the owner's x-flag position.

It sometimes happens that a program needs to be able to access data files that belong to the owner of that program, and that these data files must not have read/write permissions for other users (password data files, for example). Nevertheless, you might need other users to be able to run your program and to access the data file via the program.

```
-rwx--x--x  1  pc        staff      8113  Jun 16  09:22  changepass
-rw-------  1  pc        staff       882  Jun 16  09:25  passwords
```

As you can see from the example above, the file's owner (pc) can read and write to the **passwords** data file, and when it is being executed by the owner, the program **changepass** can also read and write **passwords.**

However, as it stands anyone else executing **changepass** (which you can see they have permission to do) would still be unable to access **passwords** as they do not have permissions for this file. What is needed to overcome this problem is to allow anyone who can execute **changepass** (everyone in this example) to operate the program as though they were its owner, and this is what the s flag in the owner x flag position indicates. By changing the permissions in the previous example as follows, anyone who can execute **changepass** can be allowed to change their own password in the **passwords** data file without being given general read/write permissions to the file.

```
-rws--x--x  1  pc        staff      8113  Jun 16  09:22  changepass
-rw-------  1  pc        staff       882  Jun 16  09:25  passwords
```

It is also possible to set an s flag in the group x flag position which will then allow any user of the program the same permissions as members of the owner's group. In the passwords example, changing the permissions on the two files to:

```
-rwx--s--x  1  pc        staff      8113  Jun 16  09:22  changepass
-rw-rw----  1  pc        staff       882  Jun 16  09:25  passwords
```

would be equally effective in resolving the passwords access problem to members of group 'staff'.

As you might have guessed, a similar situation exists on the UNIX passwords file (**/etc/passwd**) and its update program (**/bin/passwd**) where the owner is the system supervisor (called root). Try typing:

$ **ls −l /bin/passwd /etc/passwd**

to see the result on your own system.

Continuing now across the **ls −l** listing, column 2 is called the link field, and specifies from how many different places a file is referred to within the directory structure, or how many different directory entries are all linked into the same file. UNIX allows several directory entries to be linked to the same file in order to save space.

When making copies of files, it is obviously much quicker just to generate the new directory entries and then provide a link to the existing files than to copy all a file's contents from one place to another. When deleting files with multiple links, the actual file itself will not be deleted until all of the links to the file have been deleted. Keeping a back-up directory linked to your most important files is a good way to prevent accidental file deletions. You must remember, however, that since only one actual file is involved, if you change a file's contents via one of its links, then the file is changed for all.

As you have already seen, column 3 is the file owner's name and column 4 is the name of the owner's group. On some versions of UNIX the **ls** command does not supply the owner's group information unless it is specifically requested with a **−g** parameter (**ls −lg**). Column 5 represents the size of the file in characters. Following the file size is the date and time that the file was last modified or, if the date does not refer to the current year, then the date and year of last modification is given instead. The final column is obviously the file name.

Going through the **ls −l** output has probably raised several questions about files and permissions, like how to copy and link files, and how to modify the access permission flags. To copy a file, you should use the **cp** command:

$ **cp /etc/motd /usr/you/motd**

This will copy the first file named into the second file named, creating the second file if it does not already exist. Typing **ls −l /usr/you/motd** now will show a link value of 1 for the file, meaning that **/usr/you/motd** is a separate file from **/etc/motd**, even though currently they have identical contents.

In order to create a file that is linked to an existing file rather than being a copy of it, you use the **ln** command.

$ **ln /usr/you/motd /usr/you/motdlink**

will create a new directory entry called **motdlink** in your home directory which **ls −l** should show to be a linked file, with a link value of 2. As the new file is linked to **motd**, then this should also now show a link value of 2.

A third command related to **cp** and **ln** is **mv**. This command allows you to rename a file. Try:

$ **mv /usr/you/motd /usr/you/newmotd**

and **ls** should now show you that the file previously called **motd** is now named **newmotd**, but that it still has two links and is in fact just the same file renamed.

Removing files is just as easy as creating them. This is done using the **rm** command, followed by the name of the file to remove:

$ **rm /usr/you/newmotd**

will remove one link to the data file we have been using, and **ls** should now show that only one link remains (**motdlink**).

Changing a file's access permission flags is done by changing the file's access mode with the **chmod** command. In order to use **chmod** on a file, you have to be the file owner. The general form for the **chmod** command is:

$ **chmod mode filenames**

where mode is the specification of the access permission flags. There are two ways to specify the mode. The easiest is to use four octal digits. The first octal digit controls the set uid and set gid flags. The second octal digit specifies permission flags for the owner, the third digit specifies flags for the owner's group and the fourth digit is for everyone else. In order to work out what number (in the range 0–7) each digit should be, you need to give read permission and the set uid flag a value of 4, write permission and the set gid flag a value of 2 and execute/search permission a value of 1. Each digit then just becomes the sum of the values given to the permissions you wish to allow. For example, to give rwx permission to owner, rw— permission to group and ——x permission to others, the four octal digits would be; 0 for set uid/gid, rwx=4+2+1=7 for owner, rw—=4+2=6 for owner's group and ——x=1 for others. To change the mode of a file to give these permission flags, type:

$ **chmod Ø761 /usr/you/motdlink**

Now typing:

$ **ls —l /usr/you/motdlink**

should give:

—rwxrw———x

for the access permission flags as required. When specifying the octal mode value there is no need to enter leading zero digits, so the previous command line is exactly equivalent to:

$ **chmod 761 /usr/you/motdlink**

So far, all the file manipulations you have done have been in your top-level or home directory. To finish off this section it would be useful to look at how to create and delete your own subdirectories. This is something that you should get into the habit of doing in order to improve the organization of your files by keeping related files together in separate subdirectories. In order to make a new subdirectory, you use the command **mkdir**. So:

$ **cd**
$ **mkdir progs**

---

will create a directory called **progs** as a subdirectory to your home directory. You can move into the new subdirectory with the **cd** command, and add new files as we have already done in your home directory.

To delete a directory in UNIX, use the command **rmdir** followed by the name of the directory to be removed. The **rmdir** command will not work on a directory that contains any files, so all the files must be deleted first with **rm**.

2.5 COMMAND SUMMARY

Here is a list of all the commands presented in this chapter, in alphabetical order. An example of the syntax of each command is given along with a brief description. In the syntax definitions a pair of square brackets [ ] is used to enclose optional items and three dots . . . following an item indicate that the item may be repeated zero or more times.

cat	Used to concatenate and list files.
	cat file . . .
cd	Change current working directory.
	cd path
chmod	Change the access permission bits on a file or group of files. This is done by specifying the required permission bit pattern as a set of octal digits (called the mode).
	chmod mode file . . .
cp	Copy files. To copy one file on to another you should use the command line:
	cp fromfile tofile
	To copy a set of files into a directory using the existing file names:
	cp file . . . directory
ln	Given files are linked to a target file.
	ln file . . . target
ls	Gives a sorted list of directory contents.
	ls [−[l][g]] name . . .

mail   Read or send mail messages.
             mail [logname]
mesg   Enable/disable terminal messages.
             mesg [y] [n]
mkdir   Create one or more new subdirectories.
             mkdir directory ...
more   Similar to **cat** but with page breaks. At a page break,
             RETURN displays the next line, SPACE displays the next page
             and the letter 'q' quits the program.
             more file ...
mv   Same as **cp**, but moves files not copies.
             mv fromfile tofile
             mv file ... directory
passwd   Allows users to change their passwords.
             passwd
pwd   Print current working directory name.
             pwd
rm   Remove specified files from file system.
             rm file ...
rmdir   Remove specified directories from the file system. The
             directories must be empty,
             rmdir directory ...
wc   Counts words, lines and characters in files.
             wc [−[l] [w] [c]] file ...
who   Gives a list of currently logged on users.
             who
write   Allows on-line chat facilities with a specified user.
             write logname

3 | Shell basics

So far you have been led to consider quite a few basic UNIX commands, but without giving any consideration to the subject of what it is that takes and executes your commands. In fact, these functions along with many others, like printing the prompt and checking the commands you enter for syntax errors, are performed by a program that is itself a UNIX command. This program is called 'the shell'. There are several versions of the shell supplied with different versions of UNIX and its look-alikes. This book concentrates on the standard shell as distributed with UNIX system V release 2. The prompt from the standard shell is the dollar sign ($) that has appeared in the examples in Chapter 2. If you are unsure about which version of the shell you are running, then you should be able to run your system's standard shell by typing the command:

$ **/bin/sh**

Not only does the shell provide an interactive interface between UNIX and its users, but as we shall see later in this chapter and in much more detail in Chapter 6, it also provides a high-level programming language through which users can build up files of standard commands that can then be executed as though they were ordinary UNIX system commands. This allows a particular user or group of users to create an environment that is particularly suited to their needs.

3.1 I/O REDIRECTION

The basic philosophy behind the provision of UNIX facilities is to make a lot of simple commands available that perform small and specific functions efficiently. Larger and more complex commands can then be built up from the standard command set.

Many UNIX commands are designed to take their input from your terminal keyboard and to provide their output to your terminal screen. Sometimes you may prefer the output, for example, to go to a file and not to the screen. Obviously, it would be possible to write all UNIX commands in such a way that an optional extra parameter could specify the file to which program output should be sent. Similarly, optional extra parameters could specify an alternative source for program input. UNIX does not operate in this way, however, but provides facilities that allow a program's standard input and output to be redirected as required.

For example, the command:

$ ls −l >dir

would generate a sorted long listing of the contents of the current directory (as expected) but rather than send the output to your terminal screen, it would be sent to the file named **dir** in the current directory. This redirection of the program output is specified by the greater than symbol (>) on the command line followed by an alternative program output destination. The specified file will be created if it does not already exist, or emptied before writing if it does exist. You should realize that the use of the > symbol is not associated with the **ls** command, but is detected and implemented by the shell command line interpreter. This means that the standard output of any program can be redirected in this way, including command programs you write yourself.

Sometimes you may have a file that already exists to which you wish to append the output of another program. Using just the (>) standard output redirection character, this cannot be done because, as you have seen already, if you specify a file that exists after (>), then the contents of the file will be lost and overwritten with the new output. To overcome this situation and allow redirected output to be appended on to the end of an existing file, another output redirection symbol is provided:

$ ls −l / > >dir

This command line will append the sorted long listing of the root directory (/) on to the end of the existing information in the file **dir** using the append redirection operator (>>).

Just as the output from a program can be redirected, so can a program's input:

$ wc </etc/passwd

You remember that the word count command without any parameters speci-fied will count the lines, words and characters entered from the standard input device (keyboard by default) until an EOF (ctrl–d) is encountered. By use of the input redirection operator (<) standard input can be rerouted to come from a new source. In the above example, the new source is the system password file **/etc/passwd**.

I/O redirection can easily be used to perform new actions for which no standard commands exist. Suppose, for example, you wanted to know how many files were contained in your home directory, then the following command sequence would produce the required value:

```
$ cd
$ ls  > dir
$ wc −1  < dir
```

The first command changes working directory to your home directory. The second command sends a list of directory entries to a file called **dir** and the last line counts the number of lines (i.e. file names) in the file **dir** and prints this value as required. Unfortunately, the file **dir** will be created in your home directory and will thus be included in the count. If you wish to avoid this problem, then the UNIX file system provides a directory that you can use just to create temporary files. It is called **/tmp**. So the new command sequence would appear as:

```
$ cd
$ ls  > /tmp/dir
$ wc −1  < /tmp/dir
$ rm /tmp/dir
```

Notice the removal of the temporary file at the end of the command sequence. This should always be done for any files you create in **/tmp** as soon as you have finished with them. Failure to comply with this convention may well result in a mail message to you from your system administrator.

Essentially what is happening in the directory count example is that I/O redirection is being used to send the output of one command program (here **ls**) into the input of another command program (here **wc**).

3.2 PIPES

The idea of sending the output of one program into the input of another is used so often in building up new commands that UNIX provides a special mechanism for doing just this — it is called 'pipes'. Using a pipe, the previous example would appear as follows:

```
$ cd
$ ls | wc −1
```

Notice the pipe operator (vertical bar |) between the **ls** and **wc** commands. This causes the standard output of **ls** to be piped into the standard input of **wc**. The piped sequence has exactly the same effect as the previous version, except that no intermediate file (**/tmp/dir** in the example) is created or used.

Another similar example counts the number of users currently logged on to the system:

$ **who** I **wc** **−l**

This example works by piping the current list of users from **who** into the **wc** command as before, again using **−l** to count the number of lines.

3.3 MULTITASKING

As there is no intermediate file created when the pipe operator is used, this means that the two programs at each end of the pipe have to be running together at the same time so that the output of the first program can be used up by the second program as it is created. This is no problem for UNIX as it is a multitasking operating system, capable of running many processes at the same time. A UNIX command exists that will enable you to see what processes are running — type in the command:

$ **ps**

This command will produce an output like:

```
$ ps

PID     TTY     TIME    CMD
827     011     0:17    sh
901     011     0:01    ps
```

which is a list of all the processes running for you. PID is a unique process identity number generated and used by the system. TTY is the terminal from which the processes are being run, TIME is the amount of processor time that each process has used in minutes and seconds, and CMD is the name of the command being run. In order to get a list of all processes running on the system (not just your own), type:

```
$ ps −e

PID     TTY     TIME    CMD
0       ?       0:08    swapper
1       ?       0:02    init
44      011     0:08    sh
32      con     0:00    hopen
45      005     0:01    getty
74      011     0:02    ps
43      ?       0:00    lpsched
```

Notice in this output and the last you have a shell (**sh**) running at the same time as **ps**. This is due to the way that the shell actually executes the programs you give it as commands. What happens is that the shell uses a special UNIX system facility called **fork** to split itself into two identical processes. One of them (the original shell) is called the parent process and the other is called the child. These two processes are then able to run independently of each other. The child process uses another UNIX system facility called **exec** to overlay its copy of the shell with the command that you want executing. Meanwhile, the original shell in the parent process uses yet another UNIX system facility called **wait** in order to suspend its own execution. The execution of the parent process remains suspended until the child process finishes running and dies. At this time, a signal is sent via the UNIX operating system from the terminating child process to the waiting parent process to wake it up so that it may resume execution and present you with a prompt for your next command.

This explains why when you ran the **ps** command you saw that you had

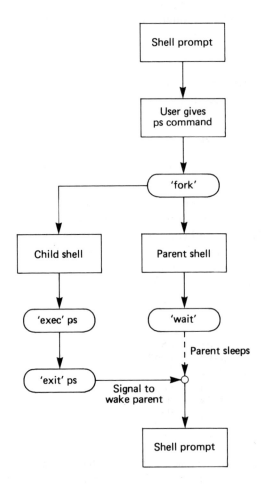

Fig. 3.1 The shell executes a command and waits for it to terminate.

two processes running. One was the child process that was running to provide you with the listing, and the other was the shell parent process waiting for its child to terminate.

By using this mechanism, UNIX ensures that the shell, in effect, executes the commands you enter as though they were subroutines so that whatever environment you have set up (like current directory, for example) it remains in force after your commands have finished.

Diagrammatically, this situation appears as in Fig. 3.1.

3.4 BACKGROUND PROCESSES

Sometimes it may happen that a particular child process produces a lot of output which it writes to a file. This means that you will have to wait quite a time before the parent process wakes up and you can type in your next command. At least, you would if UNIX did not have a facility to cater for this situation. All you have to do is to place an ampersand character (**&**) at the end of your command line. The situation will then be as in Fig. 3.2.

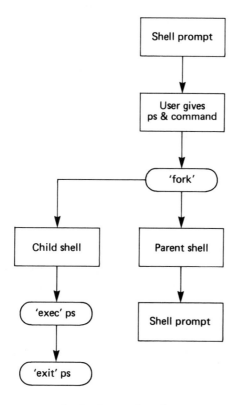

Fig. 3.2 Executing a command in background mode.

As you can see, the big difference is that when an ampersand (**&**) is appended to the end of a command line, the parent process does not execute the **wait** system call, but returns with the next shell prompt immediately. By this mechanism, it is obviously possible to have several child processes running at the same time (concurrently). Essentially, the parent shell is the foreground process, while any child processes you create execute in the background.

3.5 SHELL SCRIPTS

It has already been said that as well as providing a user command interpreter, the shell can also be used as a powerful programming language in its own right. The most obvious reason for wanting to write shell programs and the reason we shall explore first, is that very often a standard command for some application is not available, but the operation can be performed by a combination or sequence of simpler commands. You have seen examples of this in counting the number of files in your home directory, and counting the number of users currently logged on to your system. A shell program (called a shell script) can be created just by entering the required command sequence into a text file. For a simple command sequence the easiest way to enter the text into a file is with the **cat** command. You remember that **cat** with no parameters just copies its standard input to its standard output. By using output redirection, the text entered at your keyboard can be redirected straight to a file. For example,

$ cat > whocount

After this command, anything you type up to end of file will be stored in the file **whocount**. Enter the text:

who | wc — l

followed by ctrl–d to terminate the **cat** command.

3.6 EXECUTING SHELL PROGRAMS

In order to be able to execute the contents of the **whocount** file, all you have to do is to use **chmod** to set the file permissions so that the file is executable to you. This can be done with the command:

$ chmod 700 whocount

The file **whocount** can now be executed as though it was a standard UNIX command just by naming it:

$ whocount

Similarly, the following sequence would produce a command to count the files in your home directory:

```
$ cat > dircount
cd
ls | wc −1
< ctrl–d >
$ chmod 700 dircount
$ dircount
```

One special shell script that is recognized by the shell is called

.profile

This shell script is placed in your home directory and when you login the shell automatically looks for it there. If it exists then the shell will execute any commands it contains. This can be useful for setting up an initial working environment.

3.7 SHELL VARIABLES

The **dircount** command that you have just created is quite useful, but it would be much better if it could be made more general so that the number of files in any general directory could be counted. To do this, some mechanism is required that allows a parameter (here a directory name) to be passed to **dircount** which can then be used as a directory name in the **cd** command at the start of the shell script.

Most computer languages allow for the use of variables and the shell is no exception. It is by use of shell variables that you will be able to pass the required parameter. The UNIX shell provides a set of special variables called positional parameters, and given the names $1, $2, . . . From within a shell script, $1 takes as its value the first string (if any) that is entered on the command line after the command name that invoked the shell script. $2, $3, etc. then take the values of the second, third, etc. parameters on the command line. For example, suppose you invoke a shell script called **script** using the following command line:

$ script this is a test

Then from within the shell script, the positional parameter variables would be assigned as follows:

$1 − this
$2 − is
$3 − a
$4 − test

In addition to the variables $1, $2, . . ., several other variables are also set up.

$0 is set to the name of the shell script command running, i.e. script in the above example, $* is a shorthand notation that means a list of all the defined positional parameters and $# is set to the number of positional parameters (in decimal) not including $0 that have been assigned values. In the script example, $# would be set to 4, and $* would be 'this is a test'.

Within a shell script, you can use a positional parameter in any position where a normal command parameter would be used and the value of the positional parameter will be substituted into the command as its parameter value. For example, to generalize the **dircount** shell script you looked at earlier so that it will count the number of entries in any specified directory, it can be modified to:

```
cd $1
ls | wc −l
```

with the positional parameter $1 specified as the parameter to the **cd** command at the start of the shell script. If **dircount** is now invoked as follows:

$ **dircount /**

then the value / will be assigned to $1. This will cause **cd** to change directory to the root directory in this example before counting the directory entries. By this method, a file count can be made for any specified directory.

3.7.1 General shell variables

In addition to the positional parameters, the shell also allows the use of general purpose string variables. Each variable name starts with a letter or underscore which can be followed by a further sequence of zero or more letters, digits and underscore characters. Values are assigned to general shell variables by use of assignment statements of the form:

```
$ pathname=/etc/passwd
$ mydir=/usr/users/me
$ usernum=L0086900
```

Notice there are no spaces around the equals (=) sign. The value of a variable can be used as a parameter in a command just by preceding its name with a dollar ($) symbol, so that:

$ **cat $pathname**

would list the contents of the system password file using the value of the

pathname variable and:

$ cd $mydir

would change your current working directory to **/usr/users/me** if this directory exists and is open to you.

Upper- and lower-case characters are treated as distinct in variable names so that

VAR1
Var1
var1

are all separate variable names which can coexist and hold different values.

Some variables have special significance to the shell and these variables should not be used for other general purposes. The most common of the special variables and their uses are:

HOME   This variable is set up to contain the full path name to your home directory. The information in **HOME** is used by the **cd** command to determine where your home directory is when **cd** is used with no directory parameter specified. In other words the command:

$ cd

on its own is equivalent to:

$ cd $HOME

The **HOME** variable is automatically set to its correct value by the system as you logon.

MAIL   This variable is set up to be the full path name to your personal mail file. For example, if your login name is rachel, then the contents of your **MAIL** variable would be something like:

/usr/mail/rachel

Any time **MAIL** is used to send a message to you then this file will be used to store the message until you read it. The shell will periodically check the file specified in **MAIL** to see if its contents have been changed. If they have, then you will receive the message:

you have mail

as a prompt that you should use the **mail** command to read your new messages.

TERM   This variable holds the name of the systems idea of the terminal type you are using. This information is generally used by screen-based text editors.

PATH   This variable contains a list of directory names separated by colons (:). When you give the name of a command to the shell to execute, the shell needs to know where in the directory structure to look for the specified command files. It does this by using the directory names in **PATH** as a list of directories to be searched for the command. The directories are searched in the order specified in **PATH,** left to right.

If the **PATH** variable is not set up, then the command search defaults to the directories:

/bin
/usr/bin

A typical value that might be assigned to PATH is:

$ PATH=.:./bin: $HOME: $HOME/bin: /bin: /usr/bin

This specifies that six directories will be searched, starting with dot (.) and ending with **/usr/bin.** You remember from Chapter 2 that the symbol dot (.) is standard shell notation that refers to the current directory. The next directory, **./bin,** means the **bin** directory that is a child of the current directory (if one exists). This is followed by your **HOME** directory and then the **bin** child of your **HOME** directory. Finally, **/bin** and **/usr/bin** are searched as before.

Sometimes it may happen that you will want to execute a command that is not contained in your current **PATH**. In this case, you want some method of telling the shell to ignore the contents of the **PATH** variable and take a command from some other specified directory instead. This can be done by specifying the full path name to the command you want to execute:

$ /etc/chown pc file.c

Here, **chown** is a command to change ownership of a file **(file.c)** to the specified user **(pc)**. If **chown** is in the directory **/etc**, then a search through the example **PATH** will not find the command. But specifying the full path name allows the command to be executed as required. It is also possible to execute files not in the current **PATH** by specifying a relative path name, as long as there is at least one slash (/) character in the path name. This means that files in the current directory (if this is not in **PATH**) need to be specified as:

$ ./command

using the dot (.) notation to refer to the current directory.

PS1   This is the variable that holds the shell prompt which starts off as a dollar symbol ($), but which can be changed as required

$ PS1=Phil:

The shell will use the string:

Phil:

as its primary prompt string from now on.

PS2   If you press RETURN on a command line when more input is still required, then you will get the contents of **PS2** as a new prompt. The default value is a greater than symbol (>). Again this can be changed as required:

$ PS2=More:

The contents of any shell variables that are set up can be viewed by using the built-in shell command:

$ set

This produces an output like the following:

$ set
LOGNAME=pc
MAIL=/usr/mail/pc
PATH=/bin:/usr/bin:/etc:.:/usr/local/bin:
PS1=$
PS2= >
SHELL=/bin/sh
TERM=vt100
TZ=GMT0BST

3.7.2 Output from shell scripts

If you want to examine the contents of specific shell variables then rather than use **set**, which displays the contents of all variables currently set up, you should use the command **echo** followed by the variable names:

$ echo $PATH
/bin:/usr/bin:/etc:.:/usr/local/bin:

The **echo** command can also be used to output text messages as well as variable values as follows:

$ echo this is a text message

What happens here is that any words that appear after the command name (**echo**) are just repeated to the standard output device. This can be very useful for printing messages inside shell scripts. Obviously then, this example would just produce the text message:

$ echo this is a text message
this is a text message

3.8 METACHARACTERS

All the file names you have seen so far have been completely unambiguous, i.e. all the characters in the name have been specified. However, it is possible to specify an ambiguous file name to many commands and the system will sort them out. An example of an ambiguous file name is:

*t

where the asterisk (*) will match any number of characters. This example means 'all files in the current directory that end with t'. Used in a command this could be:

$ ls *t

This will list all files in the current directory whose names end in t. The asterisk is an example of a special character called a metacharacter. Another example of a metacharacter is the question mark (?) which is similar to the asterisk except that it only matches a single character. So that:

$ ls ??

will list all files in the current directory with names that are just two characters long. You should appreciate that the metacharacters are dealt with by the shell and not by the command that they are used on. This means that they can be used on any commands, even those you write yourself.

3.9 SUMMARY

3.9.1 Commands

chown	Change ownership of a file. This can only be done by the file's existing owner or the system administrator **chown newowner file ...**
echo	Print shell variable values or literal string parameter values **echo $variable ...** **echo textstring ...**
ps	Gives a list of running processes **ps [−e]**
set	Gives a list of all currently set shell variables **set**

3.9.2 Shell metacharacters

>	Output redirection (overwrite)
>>	Output redirection (append)
<	Input redirection
|	Pipe between commands
&	Run command in the background
*	Matches any characters in a file name
?	Matches a single character in a file name

3.9.3. Shell variables

$0,. .,$n	Positional parameters passed to commands
$ #	Number of positional parameters ($1 on)
$*	String of positional parameters ($1 on)
HOME	Absolute path to your home directory
MAIL	Absolute path to your mail file
TERM	Your terminal type (from /etc/ttytype)
PATH	Directories to search for a command
PS1	Main shell prompt string
PS2	Secondary shell prompt string

Editing files

4.1 THE ED EDITOR

If you have been going through this book in order, then you will probably
have wondered how to modify the contents of a text file — especially if you
made any errors typing in your shell scripts via the **cat** command and had to
retype the whole file. Fortunately, all the examples you have looked at so far
have been quite short and easy to retype, but obviously this will not always
be the case. In general, the solution to the problem of modifying the contents
of a text file is to use a text editor. The UNIX operating system provides a
standard text editor called **ed**. This editor was designed so that it can be
used on any sort of terminal from a low-speed hard-copy terminal connected
over a modem and telephone line, to a high-speed VDU terminal connected
directly to the machine. Obviously, therefore, **ed** only needs to provide facilities to enable the poorest of these terminal types to have full access to its editing power. This does mean that its methods do not take account of most of
the powerful facilities available on many modern VDU terminals. However,
ed does have advantages: it is very fast, it is quick and easy to learn, and,
most important, it is available on all UNIX systems.

4.2 CREATING A FILE

To invoke the editor, type:

$ **ed**

When you do this, it will look as though nothing is happening because **ed**
does not return a prompt. However, to convince yourself that **ed** is really
there, just press return and **ed** will respond with a question mark to tell you
it did not understand your command (which is not surprising as you did not
give it one).

  The first thing to do when creating a new file is to add some text. This can
be done with the **a** command meaning add or append text after the current
line. With a new file that is still empty, the current line is right at the start
(line 0 if you like) so that the first line added will be line 1. You should press
return at the end of each line. The editor will continue to add text to the new
file until you enter a full stop (.) on a line of its own. Key in the following
example:

```
$ ed
a
Up Jack got and home did trot
As fast as he could caper
Went to bed and wrapped his head
In vinegar and brown paper
.
```

Remember, the full stop on the line on its own at the end of the verse is not entered into the text, but is used to terminate the **a** command and return to **ed** command mode.

4.2.1 Saving text

To save text entered so far, you need the **w** command which will write a block of text from the **ed** text buffer out to a file. Type a **w** then press return. You will find that **ed** complains about this with a question mark, again to indicate it cannot comply. The reason for the question mark is that **ed** does not know what file name to use. Most commands that deal with files (including **w**) can have a file name specified after the command letter. Once a file name has been specified in one of the file commands, it is saved by **ed** and used as the default file name in other file commands when no new file name is given. To find out the current default file name, just type **f** followed by return. In the current example no default file name yet exists, and so the **f** command just returns a blank.

Now type the command:

```
w rhyme
116
```

with a space after the **w**. This will cause the entire contents of the text buffer to be written to the specified file (rhyme in this example). It will also cause the specified file name to be set up as the default file name. Notice the 116 returned by **ed**. This is a count of the number of characters written to the file. If the specified file does not exist, it will be created. If it does exist, then it will be overwritten.

Now type in the following two commands:

```
f
rhyme
w
116
```

The **f** command shows that the default file name has been set up to 'rhyme'. The **w** command will now use this default file name as the destination for its write operation. Obviously, since you have made no changes to the text, the **w** command again writes 116 characters to the file, overwriting its previous contents.

4.2.2 Leaving the editor

You can quit from the editor with the **q** command. This is a very simple command that might easily be typed by accident (instead of **w** or **a** for example). If you were to quit the editor without saving the text buffer, then any changes or additions you might have made during the session would be lost and would have to be redone. To help overcome this problem, **ed** automatically checks to see if any changes have been made to the buffer since it was last saved. If there are changes, then a question mark is output as a reminder. If you really do not want to save the buffer, then giving the **q** command for a second time straight after the first will quit the editor as you intended. You can also quit the editor without any of the normal checks by using the command **Q** instead of **q**.

4.2.3 Adding more text

When you have quit the editor, type in the command:

```
$ wc rhyme
   4   25   116   rhyme
```

---

showing that you have created a file called **rhyme** consisting of 4 lines, 25 words and 116 characters as expected.

Now type the command:

```
$ ed rhyme
116
```

As you have specified a file name on the command line **ed** automatically makes this the default file name. Because the file name exists in this example, **ed** reads the file contents into its text buffer and tells you it has done so by printing a count of the file length (116 again). If the file did not exist then you would get the now familiar question mark from **ed** followed by your specified file name as follows:

```
$ ed nofile
? nofile
```

This would be the output assuming that the file **nofile** did not exist. Note that **nofile** would still be made the default file name.

Going back to 'rhyme' now, **ed** has just told you that it is loaded into the text buffer and is ready for further editing. To add more text after the end of the existing verse use the **a** command again:

```
$ ed rhyme
116
a
When Jill came in how she did grin
To see Jack's head in plaster
Her mother vexed did scold her next
For causing Jack's disaster
.
```

Notice once again that the full stop (.) is used on a line on its own to terminate the additions and return to command mode.

4.3 LISTING THE FILE

Having got all this text in, it would be useful to be able to see it. A line of the file can be printed on the terminal with a **p** command. Try it:

```
p
For causing Jack's disaster
```

Each time you give the **p** command, it will print out this single line. This is because unless you specify otherwise, most commands in **ed** use a default line number. In the current example, the default line number is 8. It was set up by the previous **a** command as the number of the last line you added. To print a different line, you just precede the **p** command by the number of the line you wish to print:

1p
Up Jack got and home did trot
2p
As fast as he could caper
p
As fast as he could caper

Notice that as a side-effect the default line number is updated to the number of the line printed.

4.3.1 Line number ranges

It soon gets quite tedious printing quantities of text by this method. To overcome the problem, you can also specify a range of line numbers to which the command then refers:

4,6p
In vinegar and brown paper
When Jill came in how she did grin
To see Jack's head in plaster
p
To see Jack's head in plaster

Here, lines 4–6 inclusive have been printed. Notice that the default line number has been set to the number of the last line printed.

In this example it would be possible to print the rest of the text with the command line **6,8p** because you know the current line is 6 and the last line is 8. If you did not have this information, it would still be possible to print this section of text using two special characters. The dot symbol (.) is the character that means the current default line, and the dollar symbol ($) is the character that means the line number of the last line in the buffer. To find out the current values of dot and dollar (the default and last line numbers) you can use the commands:

.=
6
$=
8

---

showing the current values to be 6 and 8 respectively.

Dot and dollar can also be used directly as required:

.,$p
To see Jack's head in plaster
Her mother vexed did scold her next
For causing Jack's disaster

This technique of specifying a line number or range of line numbers before a command can be used with most commands if it would make sense. So that

---

5,$w rhyme2
129

---

creates a file called rhyme2 and writes the last verse (lines 5 to $) of Jack and Jill into it, which is 129 characters long.

Obviously, then, using the **w** command on its own is equivalent to:

1,$w

i.e. it writes away the whole buffer from line 1 to the end.

4.3.2 Inserting lines in the text

A starting line number can also be used with the **a** command so that **3a** means add text after line 3. The **a** on its own is equivalent to **.a**, i.e. add text after the current default line.   As well as adding text after a line, it is also possible to insert text before a line using the **i** command. The first verse of Jack and Jill can be added as follows:

1i
Jack and Jill
Jack and Jill went up the hill
To fetch a pail of water
Jack fell down and broke his crown
And Jill came tumbling after
.

Notice that **i** is terminated with a full stop just like **a**.

If you list the whole rhyme now with **1,$p** you will find a block of text that is not laid out very well — the title and the individual verses could do with separating out a bit. However, to insert blank lines in the text you need to know the line numbers of the places to add the blanks. This can be done by listing the text with the **n** command to number the lines instead of using **p** as follows:

1,$n

From this you will find that blank lines need to be added after lines 1, 5 and 9. In this case it will be better to insert the blank lines in the order 9, 5, 1. Otherwise, inserting a line early on in the text will cause later line numbers to change.

At this point, your text should appear as follows:

1,$n
1   Jack and Jill
2
3   Jack and Jill _____
4   _____
15   _____
16   For causing Jack's disaster

4.3.3 Deleting lines

If you made any errors while entering the text, but you did not notice until after you pressed return on the line, then you may have a line or lines that you want to delete. You do this with the **d** command:

d

deletes the current default line (equivalent to **.d**)

6d

deletes line 6

3,7d

deletes lines 3–7 inclusive, and so on.

After the delete, the current default line number (which you remember can be viewed with the command **.=**) will be set either to the lowest line number deleted or the new value of $, whichever is smaller.

Another way to delete a block of text if you intend to change it for something else is to use the **c** command:

6,8c

lets you change lines 6–8 into something else and is equivalent to:

6,8d
i

4.3.4 Cut and paste operations

Sometimes you do not want to delete a block of text, you just want to move it to somewhere else in the document. The **m** command serves this purpose:

2,6m$

takes the contents of lines 2–6 inclusive (i.e. the first verse) and moves this block to the end of the text. This means that there is still only one copy of the five lines that were moved, but they now occur at the end instead of the beginning. A similar command allows you to transfer a copy of a block of text so that multiple copies can exist — the **t** command:

12,$t1

takes a copy of the moved first verse from the end of the rhyme and puts it back where it belongs. Two copies of verse one now exist, one at the start and one at the end.

4.4 FINDING LINES

So far, you have only referred to lines by their line numbers. These can be used to set the default current line just by specifying the required number. So giving as a command:

8

would set the default line to 8 and cause the line to be printed (so that **8** and **8p** are equivalent).

The default current line can also be set up by specifying a string of characters to find within the text and using the number of the line on which the string is first found. To do this, the required string just needs to be enclosed within a pair of slash (/) or question mark (?) characters:

/Up/
Up Jack got and home did trot
.=
8

The search always begins at the current default line which is updated when a match is found. When the slash characters are used to enclose the string, the search proceeds from the default line forwards through the text. When the question mark is used, the search is conducted backwards towards line 1. When the limit of the text is reached in either direction, the search wraps around the text buffer and continues on from the other end. For example, when line 1 is reached in a backward search, the next line to be scanned is $.

The line numbers generated by string searches can be used in commands in just the same way as ordinary numbers:

/Up/,$w lastbit
246

This command line will write a block of text to the file **lastbit**. The block written starts at the first line found to contain the string **Up** (i.e. line 8) and continues until the end of the text buffer. In this case, the last two verses are written to the file lastbit, which **ed** tells you are 246 characters long.

As there is only one line containing the string **Up** it does not matter where the search starts from, or in which direction. Sometimes it can matter (looking for the string **and** for example) and you will need to specify a start value for the default line number before the search begins. Having found one occurrence of a string, the next occurrence can be found quite simply:

7
/and/
Up Jack got and home did trot
//
Went to bed and wrapped his head
//
In vinegar and brown paper

When two dashes (**//**) or two question marks (**??**) are specified with no contents, then the previously specified search string is used by default.

One problem to watch for is as follows. Suppose the current default line number is 7 and you want to print the first three lines of verse 1 — you might try:

?hill?,/his/n

to search back from line 7 to find **hill** in line 3 and then forward from line 3 to find **his** in line 5, printing between lines 3 and 5 as required. However, what you actually get is from **hill** in line 3 to **his** in line 10 as both searches take place from the default line 7. To overcome this problem, you use a semi-colon (**;**) instead of a comma (**,**) in the command line which tells **ed** to update the default line number after each search:

?hill?;/his/n
3   Jack and Jill _____
4   To fetch a pail _____
5   Jack fell _____

4.4.1 Line number expressions

In working out line numbers, it is also possible to include simple numeric expressions using addition or subtraction. Try the following:

$−2,$n

prints out the last three lines of the text buffer with line numbers printed as well.

.−2,.+1d

deletes four lines starting two lines back from the current line and ending one line forward of the current line.

/Up/−1;/In/+1w verse2

will write out lines 7–12 inclusive from the rhyme example to the file **verse2**.

4.5 FILE HANDLING

There are several file-handling commands in ed, two of which you have seen before. The **f** command allows you to see the default work file name. If the **f** command is followed by the name of a file as in:

f rhyme

then the default file name is set to the file name specified.

The other file command you have seen is **w** which will write lines from the text buffer to a file. A line number range can be specified to restrict the quantity of information written. If a specific file name is not given, then the default file name is used. If the file name does not exist, then the file will be created. If the file does exist, then its existing contents are overwritten. If you want to edit a new file or re-edit the existing file, then the **e** command is the one to use:

e filename

erases the contents of the current text buffer and loads the contents of the specified file into **ed**. If no file name is specified, then the default file name is used. If any editing has taken place in the current text buffer since it was last written to a file, then **ed** will give its question mark error message and the **e** command will have to be repeated a second time before it becomes effective (as with **q** to quit). The **E** command is the same as **e** but does not make this safety check.

The final file command allows a file to be read into the existing text buffer contents and merged with it. This is the **r** command:

r filename

Here the contents of the specified file will be appended on to the end of the current text buffer contents. The **r** command may optionally be preceded by a line number, in which case the contents of the file are added after the specified line in the current text and not at the end. If no file name is given, the default file name is used.

4.6 SUBSTITUTION

Everything you have seen so far can be classified as operations on whole lines of text. Sometimes it would be most useful not to have to retype a long line when only a few characters need to be changed. In **ed**, the **s** command is the way to substitute one string of characters for another on the current default line. For example, to find the character **J** on a line and substitute a **T** for it:

s/J/T/

Applying this in the following example gives:

1
Jack and Jill
s/J/T/
p
Tack and Jill

Notice that only the first occurrence has been changed. To make the changes globally throughout the line, a **g** needs to be appended to the end of the command line:

1
Jack and Jill
s/J/T/gp
Tack and Till

Notice that the **p** can also be appended to the end to see the result.

Just as with other commands, a range of line numbers may be specified. The command line:

1,$s/Jack/Bill/g

will completely rewrite the rhyme to talk about Bill and Jill!

If a substitution command does not do what you expected, you can undo its effects with the **u** command.

4.7 REGULAR EXPRESSIONS

Within **ed** there are several characters that have a special meaning when they appear in a search string or in the left-hand string of an **s** command. A regular expression is a string that uses one or more of these special characters. The characters themselves are called metacharacters and they are used to make searches and substitutions more powerful.

As you have already seen, the command:

/string/

will search for and print the first occurrence of a line containing the specified string. In this case, the specified string may appear anywhere on the line. If you wanted to find a line that started with a given string rather than just contained the string, it can be done with the metacharacter ^ which stands for the beginning of the line:

/^ Jack/

This means find the first line that has the beginning of the line immediately followed by the word Jack. If you wished to find all such lines then another version of the global command **g** would be placed at the start of the line:

---

g/^ Jack/n
1   Jack and Jill
2   Jack and Jill went up the hill
5   Jack fell down and broke his crown

Notice that with this version of the **g** command any lines found can be passed on to any of the other commands (**n** in this example) just by adding the other command to the end of the line.

Just as the start of the line can be matched, so also can the end of a line with the metacharacter dollar (**$**):

---

g/aper$/n
9   As fast as he could caper
11   In vinegar and brown paper

This search finds all lines that contain the string **aper** immediately before the end of the line.

These two metacharacters can also be combined to find empty lines, i.e. lines that have a line beginning, immediately followed by a line end:

---

g/^ $/n
2
7
12

Sometimes you will want to perform a search for a string, but with any character in one of the character positions. This situation might arise with a set of product numbers for example like:

ma1d, ma2d, mb1d, mc1d

ma1b, ma3d, ma2c, ma4d

Suppose here that you wanted to search for lines containing sales of products ma1d, ma2d, ma3d and ma4d. This could obviously be done with four separate searches of the type:

g/ma1d/n
g/ma2d/n etc.

But using the metacharacter dot (.) a single search could be made to suffice:

g/ma.d/n

The dot metacharacter allows any character to match in the position where it is given (here 1, 2, 3 or 4 in the third position of the string).
Another example from the rhyme might be as follows:

---

g/a.er$/n
4   To fetch a pail of water
9   As fast as he could caper
11   In vinegar and brown paper

Here ed has been asked to print any line that ends with **a.er** where any character will do for the dot. As you can see, three matches have been found in the words **water**, **caper** and **paper**.
Going back now to the product numbers, suppose you only wanted to list products ma1d, ma2d and ma4d. What you really need now is some way to specify what are the acceptable alternatives in that third character position. This is catered for in ed by enclosing choice characters from which one must be selected inside the square bracket metacharacters **[ ]**:

g/ma[124]d/n

would perform the required operation. In the rhyme example the same idea can also be used to sort out words with upper- and lower-case letter problems:

g/[Uu]p/n
3   Jack and Jill went up the hill
8   Up Jack got and home did trot

Here the word **up** has been found either with or without an initial capital letter.

Sometimes, there may be a range of acceptable characters that would be tedious to list (say any digit from 0 to 9). These can be specified as a range:

g/ma[0—9]d/n

This would be equivalent to:

g/ma[0123456789]d/n

If the list or range of acceptable characters is very large, it may be easier to give the characters that are not acceptable:

g/ma[^ 0—9]d/n

This time only the characters 0 to 9 are not acceptable. The ^ as the first character inside the square bracket specifies this negation of meaning.

Finally, suppose that you wanted to search the rhyme example for all lines that start with **To** and end with **ster**. There is only one such line, though two lines begin with **To** (4 and 14) and two lines end with **ster** (14 and 16). How shall we find the one line when we do not even know how long it is? (Without cheating!)

What you need is a method of matching a section of a line containing unknown characters in unknown quantity.

You can already match a single unknown character with a dot. All that is needed is a way to say that there is an unspecified number of them. This is done with the metacharacter asterisk (*). So that:

/.*/

will match any number of unspecified characters. In fact, the asterisk (*) affects the preceding character in this way whatever it is:

/a*/

means an unspecified number of the character **a** (including zero!) and:

/[0—9]*/

means zero or more digits:

/[0—9][0—9]*/

means at least one digit, i.e. a digit 0—9 followed by zero or more further digits 0—9. The solution to the previous problems can now be found — it is:

---

g/ˆ To.*ster$/n
14   To see Jack's head in plaster

This means globally find and print lines that start with **To**, end with **ster** and have an unspecified amount of anything else in the middle — just as required!

Incidentally, sometimes you may wish to deal with all lines not containing a particular regular expression rather than those that do contain it. This can be specified by changing the initial **g** into a **v**:

v/Jack/n

prints out all lines with their line numbers, that do not contain the word **Jack**.

Finally it should be noted that you may occasionally want to include one or more of the metacharacters in the search string as characters to search for in their own right. This can be done by preceding the metacharacter with a backslash character (\):

g/*/n

This will search for the two-character sequence backslash asterisk (*). Notice here that to search for a backslash (\), the character itself also has to be preceded by a backslash.

4.8 ED COMMAND SUMMARY

4.8.1 Commands

a	Add new text until a line is entered containing just a dot (.)
c	Change a specified block of lines for new text. Equivalent to the **d** command followed by the **a** command
d	Delete a line or block of lines
e file	Start a new editing session with the specified file. Checks to see that current text buffer has been saved
E file	Same as **e** except no checks made
f file	Display or set up current default file name
g/str/cmd	Globally find lines containing 'str' and pass them on to the specified command (**cmd**)
i	Insert new text before specified line until a line is entered containing just a dot (.)
m line	Moves a specified block of lines from its current position in the text to after the specified 'line'
p	Print specified lines
q	Quit from ed. Checks to see that current text buffer has been saved

Q   Same as **q** except no checks made
r file   Read contents of **file** into the text buffers after the specified line number (or end of buffer if no line given)
s/str/new/ Substitute first occurrence of **str** with **new**. Adding **g** to the end will substitute all occurrences on the line
t line   Transfers a copy of a block of lines to after the specified **line**
u   Undo last substitution
v/str/cmd Perform the specified command (and) on all lines that do not contain the regular expression **str**
w file   Write lines of text from the text buffer to the specified file
.=   Print current default line number
$=   Print current last line number
num   Where **num** is any current line number, prints contents of line. Also sets default line to **num**
/str/   Using a forward search, find and print the next line containing the regular expression **str**
?str?   Using a backward search, find and print the next line containing the regular expression **str**

Most commands can have a line or range of lines specified over which they will operate as follows:

cmd   Perform command (**cmd**) on the current default line number
line cmd   Perform command (**cmd**) on the specified **line**
start,end Perform command (**cmd**) beginning at line **start** and finishing at line **end**

4.8.2 Metacharacters (can be used in **str**)

^   Matches the start of the line when ^ occurs at the beginning of **str**
$ Matches the end of the line when $ occurs at the end of **str**
.   Matches any single character
[]   Contains a list of characters, including ranges, any one of which may be matched
[^]   When the bracket contents start with ^ any single character other than those listed will be matched
*   The preceding single character may be matched zero or more times

4.9 EDITING FILES WITH VI

The text editor **ed** is a good all round general purpose editor that can be used in all situations. However, most modern terminals are VDU types that have some built-in capabilities to allow extra functions to be performed, such as moving the cursor on the screen to any desired position or inserting blank lines or deleting lines of text from the screen. With facilities like these available it is possible for a text editor to treat the VDU screen as though it were a window on to a small section of the internally stored text buffer. The user can then be allowed to move the text window around the contents of the text buffer and on any particular screen full of text move a cursor around the text making changes and additions as required. At all times the user has a complete view of what is happening as changes and additions are made. The standard UNIX visual window editor is called **vi**. As you may imagine, if **vi** is going to drive the special features of a particular terminal then it needs to be told the type of terminal you are using. This is done via the shell variable **TERM**. This variable can be set up in your **.profile** or from the keyboard by typing:

TERM=vt52;export TERM

After your terminal type has been set up, you can run the editor just by typing its name, followed by the name of a file to work on:

$ vi filename

If the specified file does not exist then it will be created. If it does exist then it will be read and the first screenful displayed on your terminal screen:

$ vi rhyme
Jack and Jill
Jack and Jill

_____

_____

_____

For causing Jack's disaster
~
 ~
 ~
 ~
 ~
 ~
'rhyme' 16 lines, 382 characters

As this particular file is less than one screenful in length the end of the file can be seen as well as the start. At the end of the file, unused lines are displayed as ~. The bottom line of the display is used to give error and text messages and is also the line where some of the commands you give are echoed. When **vi** is first entered, this line gives information about the name and size of the file you will be editing. The whole philosophy behind using a screen editor like **vi** is different from the use of a line editor like **ed**. With a screen editor the important things are moving the displayed window about the stored text, moving the screen cursor about the displayed window and inserting and deleting characters and lines around the current displayed cursor position.

The vi editor has three modes of operation that I shall call command mode, edit mode and insert mode. When **vi** is first invoked, you will automatically be working in edit mode. The most useful edit mode functions are as given in the headings below.

4.10 WINDOW MOVEMENT

ctrl–f   Pressing the 'control' and 'f' keys together moves the editor window forward through the text by one screenful

ctrl–b   Moves the editor window backwards through the text by one screenful

ctrl–d   Scroll the editor window down the text by half a screenful, i.e. in the same direction as **ctrl–f**

ctrl–u   Scroll the window up the text by half a screen, i.e. in the same direction as **ctrl–b**

Most of the functions used in edit mode can be preceded by a number which specifies in some way how many times to apply the function. In the case of ctrl–f and ctrl–b, if a number is given it refers to the number of screenfuls of text to skip. With ctrl–d and ctrl–u it gives the number of lines of text by which to scroll. Also note that in general, the keys you press when invoking edit mode functions are not echoed to the screen.

4.10.1 Cursor movement

It is also possible from within edit mode to move the cursor around the text window on the screen as follows:

j   Moves cursor down one line
k   Moves cursor up one line
h   Moves cursor left one character
l   Moves cursor right one character
Ø (zero)   Moves cursor to start of line
$ Moves cursor to end of line
b   Moves cursor left one word
w   Moves cursor right one word

If you try to move the cursor past the top or bottom of the screen then the window will be moved through the text to keep the cursor on screen. A number specified before one of these functions will cause the cursor to move by that number of lines, characters or words as appropriate.

4.10.2 Deleting text

Having got the cursor where you want it, you now need to be able to delete and insert text. The common delete functions in edit mode are:

dd	Pressing the 'd' key twice deletes the whole line that the cursor is sitting on, regardless of where on the line the cursor appears
dw	This will delete text from the current cursor position up to the start of the next word encountered
d$	This deletes all text from the current cursor position to the end of the current line
dØ	Deletes all text on the current line that is to the left of the cursor position
x	Deletes the single character that the cursor is sitting on

Specifying a number before **dd**, **dw** or **x** gives the number of lines, words or characters respectively that are to be deleted.

Just in case you made an error, vi copies any text that you delete into a temporary buffer before it is deleted. Remember that there is only one such buffer so that only one block of deleted text (the latest block) can be stored.

4.10.3 Restoring deleted text

To restore the last block of text if it was deleted in error just requires that the temporary save buffer be copied back into the current text buffer.

p	Copies the temporary buffer directly after the current cursor position
P	Copies the temporary buffer directly before the current cursor position

This technique can also be used to duplicate a line by deleting it with **dd** and then restoring it twice with **PP**.

4.10.4 Insert mode

There are several edit mode functions that allow the transition to be made between edit mode and insert mode. When you are in insert mode all the characters you type are displayed within the screen window and are entered into the text buffer. Remember that in edit mode the characters you enter do not appear on the screen or in the text buffer but are interpreted as functions to perform. To get back from insert mode to edit mode you should press the escape key (ESC). On some terminals without an escape key you should press its equivalent, ctrl–[(i.e. control and open square bracket together). If at any time you are not sure what mode you are in all you need to do is to press escape several times until the bell sounds on your terminal (assuming it has a bell). At this point you will be in edit mode and can proceed from there.

The common insert commands are:

i	Enter insert mode and insert any subsequently typed text directly before the current cursor position. Remember to terminate with escape
a	Same as **i** except that the text is inserted after the current cursor position
o	Opens a gap in the text on the line after the current cursor line and enters insert mode with the cursor at the start of the new blank line
O	Same as **o** except that the gap is opened up on the line before the current cursor line
I	Same as **i** except insert at the start of the current cursor line
A	Same as **a** except insert after the end of the current cursor line

4.11 COMMAND MODE

Command mode is entered from edit mode by typing a colon (**:**). You can tell when you are in command mode because the bottom line of the screen contains a colon followed by the cursor on an otherwise blank line. To return to edit mode without entering a command, just press 'return'. Normally you are automatically returned to edit mode at the end of each command. In command mode, many of the facilities you encountered in **ed** are available, such as moving the cursor to specific lines just by giving the line number or moving the cursor to a line containing a string specified between slash (**/** or question mark (**?**) characters.

:/Jack/

would search forward from the current cursor position in the text to find the string 'Jack'.

:?Jill?

would search backwards through the text for the string 'Jill'.

When the specified string is found, edit mode is re-entered with the cursor sitting at the start of the required string.

4.11.1 Find and replace

This is done in just the same way as in **ed** using commands like the following:

:s/Jack/Bill/

substitutes the word 'Bill' for the first occurrence of 'Jack' on the current cursor line.

:s/Jack/Bill/g

globally substitutes 'Bill' for 'Jack' throughout the current line.

:g/Jack/s//Bill/g

globally substitutes 'Bill' for 'Jack' throughout the entire file.

4.12 FILE COMMANDS

Again the commands are similar to **ed** but not quite the same!

:w file	Write the contents of the text buffer to the specified 'file' or to the default file if none specified
:e file	Discard current text if any and start editing specified 'file'. This command will not discard the current text if it has been modified since it was last saved
:e! file	Same as **e** except no check of current text mode
:r file	Read the contents of the specified 'file' into the text buffer at the current cursor position

4.12.1 Leaving vi

This is done in one of several ways, all from within command mode:

:q	This is the method to use when you just wish to quit from **vi** without saving the current text buffer. However, the method only works if the text buffer has not been changed since it was last saved
:q!	This is the same as **q**, but it performs no checks on the save state of the current text buffer contents (i.e. quit really!)
:x	Writes out the text buffer to the default file and then quits. This is the same as **:wq**

The **vi** editor provides many more facilities than those described here, all of which are detailed in section (1) of the UNIX manual. However, the facilities detailed are those that you will require for the majority of your editing work on text and 'c' program files.

4.13 VI COMMAND SUMMARY

4.13.1 Edit mode

ctrl–f	Move window on one screen
ctrl–b	Move window back one screen
ctrl–d	Move window on half-screen
ctrl–u	Move window back half-screen
j	Moves cursor down one line
k	Moves cursor up one line
h	Moves cursor left one character
l	Moves cursor right one character
0	Moves cursor to start of line
$	Moves cursor to end of line
b	Moves cursor left one word
w	Moves cursor right one word
dd	Deletes current cursor line
dw	Delete from cursor to start of next word
d$	Delete to end of line
d0	Delete to start of line
x	Delete current character
p	Restore saved buffer after cursor
P	Restore saved buffer before cursor

4.13.2 Insert mode

i	Enter insert mode before current cursor
a	Enter insert mode after current cursor
o	Open a line after current cursor and enter insert mode on the blank line
O	Open a line before current cursor and enter insert mode on the blank line
I	Enter insert mode at start of current cursor line
A	Enter insert mode after end of current cursor line

4.13.3 Command mode

:/text/	Search forward to find 'text'
:?text?	Search backward to find 'text'
:s/t1/t2/	Substitute the first 't2' for 't1' on the current line
:s/t1/t2/g	Substitute every 't2' for 't1' on the current line
:g/t1/s//t2/g	Globally substitute 't2' for 't1' throughout the file

:w file	Write text buffer to 'file'
:e file	Discard current buffer if unchanged and load specified 'file'
:e! file	Discard current buffer and load specified 'file'
:r file	Read 'file' into buffer at current cursor position
:q	Quit **vi** if buffer unchanged
:q!	Quit **vi** without saving buffer
:x	Save buffer and quit (like **:wq**)

UNIX utilities

5

There are many situations when you may want to be able to examine and modify the contents of a file in ways that are not always suitable for the use of a straightforward text editor. This may be either because the time taken to load and use an editor is too great for some simple operations, or because the text editor does not provide automatic facilities to do some of the more sophisticated manipulations you may wish to perform. Either way UNIX provides some very powerful file manipulation utilities to give access to a whole range of these useful facilities.

5.1 FINDING STRINGS

The name **grep** stands for General Regular Expression Parser. Parsing in a computing context just means scanning text for particular string patterns. Regular expressions you have already encountered before in Chapter 4 on **ed**. You remember that they are just the types of string patterns that **ed** can search for. So **grep** then is a UNIX utility which can search for and find general regular expressions. Input to **grep** can come from a file or from the standard input device. This also means that text can be redirected into **grep** from a pipe for example. The output from **grep** consists of any lines of text that contain the specified regular expression string. These lines are listed on the standard output device and so again can easily be redirected. Here is a simple example of **grep** in use:

$ **grep root /etc/passwd**
root:fv./d4LQu5rrs:0:0::/:/bin/sh

Here **grep** is told to search the file '/etc/passwd' for the regular expression 'root'. It is also acceptable to specify a list of files on the command line which **grep** will search in turn for the specified regular expression:

```
$ grep -n getchar *.c
master.c:124:       while ((c = getchar()) ! = '/n') {
slave.c:11:         c = getchar();
```

Here all files with names ending in **.c** are searched for the string **getchar**. In cases where more than one file is to be searched the file name is added at the start of the line, followed by a colon for each match with the regular expression.

If the **−n** parameter is given then each match printed is preceded with its line number in the file.

Finding function names or variable names in C programs is a typical use for grep but others will be explored in Chapter 6.

5.2 CHARACTER TRANSLATION

The command available in UNIX to provide character translation facilities is called **tr**. The most common type of translation you might wish to perform is to convert upper-case letters in a file to lower case or vice versa.

The **tr** command is arranged, like most UNIX tools, to take its input from the standard input device and send its output to the standard output device. This makes it easy to pipe things into and out of **tr** and to redirect its input from or output to files.

The usual format of the command is:

$ tr string1 string2

where string1 and string2 are character strings of equal length. In this format, input characters in string1 are translated into the corresponding characters in string2. For example:

$ tr ab yz < trfile

Here 'ab' is string1 and 'yz' is string2. What the command line does is to take its input from the file trfile by redirection. Each occurrence of the letter 'a' in the input is translated into a letter 'y' and the letter 'b' is translated into the letter 'z'. As there is no output redirection specified in the example, the output will be sent to the terminal screen.

To translate upper-case letters to lower case the following command would work even though it would be quite tedious to type:

$ tr ABCDEFGHIJKLMNOPQRSTUVWXYZ abcdefghijklmno pqrstuvwxyz

Where ranges of characters are involved as in the last example they can be abbreviated between square brackets as follows:

$ tr [A–Z] [a–z]

This example still translates upper-case letters to lower case as before.

Any character strings used for string1 or string2 that contain characters treated as special by the shell should be enclosed in single or double quotes. Any character can be entered into string1 or string2 even those not normally printable by using the backslash character (\) followed by one, two or three octal digits, where the octal value is the ASCII code of the required character. For example to translate newline characters into spaces:

$ tr '\12' ' '

where '12' is the octal value of the ASCII code for newline.

5.3 SORTING FILE CONTENTS

There are many occasions where you may wish to sort the contents of a file into some specified order. In the UNIX environment the standard command to perform sorting operations is called **sort**. This command takes lines of text from its standard input and sorts them according to some simple rules that you can specify. The resulting lines of text are then sent to sort's standard output. By default the whole of each input line is taken as the sort key and the comparisons are made according to the order of the machine's underlying character set. In the most popular character code (ASCII) this means that the space character comes first, followed by some punctuation symbols, then the digits 0–9, then the upper-case letters A–Z and finally the lower-case letters a–z. This gives a rather strange ordering of lines if some start with upper-case letters and some with lower case, as all the lines that start with upper-case letters will be listed before all the lines that start with lower-case letters. You will see the solution to this problem later. As an example the command line:

$ sort </etc/passwd

will sort the lines of the system password file and send the sorted listing to your terminal screen. As the lines of the password file begin with users' login names, then in effect the file will be sorted into ascending user name order.

Even though this default action will suffice in a lot of cases, there are equally many situations when this is just not what is required. For these occasions sort provides a comprehensive set of options and parameters which allow sorting operations to be carried out on almost any set of conditions imaginable. For example, suppose you have a text file with line numbers and you want to sort the file into line number order:

```
5 FOR X=1 TO 10

20 PRINT X

100 NEXT X
```

Here is a trivial program written in BASIC, a language that requires line numbers. On the face of it these lines would seem to be in order already. However, if the file containing those lines is called 'basprog' in the current directory then the command:

$ sort <basprog

would produce the output:

```
$ sort <basprog

100 NEXT X

20 PRINT X

5 FOR X=1 TO 10
```

to the terminal screen. So what went wrong? Well, nothing really, **sort** normally does its comparisons to determine the order of lines a character at a time. Only if the first characters are the same will the second characters normally be considered and so on. By this rule it is obvious that 1 comes before 2, which both come before 5. So line number order 100, 20, 5 is really to be expected, even if it is not what you want. The way round the problem is to specify the **−n** option to tell **sort** to treat the sort key as numeric values:

$ sort −n < basprog

Other useful options include:

−d   The default action of **sort** considers all characters on a line as significant. With **−d** specified **sort** only considers letters, digits, spaces and tab characters

−f   This is the option that allows upper- and lower-case letters to be treated as the same thing so that upper- and lower-case key values are properly merged together rather than separated out

−r   Reverse the direction of the sort, i.e. sort in descending numeric and character order instead of the normal ascending sort order

The default sort action takes the whole line into consideration. This can be altered so that only a single field is considered and this need not be the first field either. When fields are specified the default field separator is a space or a tab. If you wish to alter the default separator you can use the option:

−tc   Where the character c will be used as the new field separator

The only thing to consider now is how to specify which field you want to refer to. Sadly, this is far from obvious and could certainly be made a lot easier. The notation uses a plus sign followed by a number. This number is the number of fields to skip to get to the key field.

$ **sort** +3n <filename

directs **sort** to perform numeric sorting of 'filename' starting on field 4.

As well as telling **sort** which field to start on it is also possible to tell it after this at which field to stop.

$ **sort** +1 −2 +6 −7 <filename

This example tells **sort** to order the lines of 'filename' based on the contents of field 2. If two or more lines are found with the same value in field 2 then field 7 will be used to order these lines.

It is, of course, always possible that two lines will be the same as far as **sort** can tell. In these cases specifying the **−u** option tells **sort** to leave only one unique copy of each line.

5.4 JOINING TWO FILES TOGETHER

Once you have the ability to sort files into order it is then possible to take two files with a common field and join them together. For example, suppose you have a file specifying the grades of workers in a factory and the weekly pay for each grade. Similarly suppose that a second file exists with factory grades and names of workers of each grade. To join the two files together they both need to be sorted into worker grade order. If the two files have the following contents:

grade1 117.26

grade2 144.22

grade3 176.86

grade4 209.43

grade5 243.78

for file1 and:

grade1 Jones DW

grade1 Smith PA

grade3 Jones PE

grade4 Davies A

grade4 Williams S

for file2, then the command:

$ **join file1 file2**

would give the output:

$ **join file1 file2**

grade1 117.26 Jones DW

grade1 117.26 Smith PA

grade3 176.86 Jones PE

grade4 209.43 Davies A

grade4 209.43 Williams S

What has happened here is that lines in the two files that contain the same values in the key fields have been combined to make all the relevant information available on each line.

In general the lines of output are laid out starting with the key field. This is followed by the rest of the fields in the first file specified and finally the rest of the fields in the second file specified.

If you do not require all the fields of both files to be printed then you can specify a list of which fields will be printed from each file and in what order. If for instance in the previous example you just wanted a list of names followed by salary values this could be done as:

$ join −o 2.2 1.2 file1 file2

using the **−o** option. What this command line means is that field 2 from file2 should be printed followed by field 2 from file1. In general:

n.m

means field m from file n. The output in this case would be:

Jones DW 117.26

Smith PA 117.26

Jones PE 176.86

Davies A 209.43

Williams S 209.43

The default field separator for **join** is a space or a tab. As with **sort** the **join** field separator can be changed with the **−tc** option where **c** is the new separator.

5.5 FINDING COMMON LINES

The **join** command is not the only operation that can be performed on two sorted files. Another possibility is **comm**. What this does is to give output in three columns. The first column contains lines that appear in the first file but not in the second. The second column contains lines appearing in the second file but not in the first. And the final column contains lines that are common to both files. If these three columns are numbered 1, 2 and 3 then any of the columns can be suppressed by giving its number as a parameter to **comm** preceded by a minus sign.

$ comm −12 file1 file2

will print only lines that are common to both files while:

$ **comm −13 file1 file2**

will only print lines that appear in file2 but not in file1.

5.6 GENERAL FILE COMPARISON

If you just want to know if the contents of two files are the same or not then the **cmp** command can be used.

$ **cmp file1 file2**

If both file1 and file2 are identical, then **cmp** will produce no output. If the two files are not the same then the byte number and the line number of the first difference discovered between the two files will be printed.

5.7 EDITING INLINE

It sometimes happens that you want to edit the contents of some text that may only exist in a pipeline between two other programs, or that you want to write a shell script that can perform some editing functions on a temporary file created and deleted during the execution of the script.

Undoubtedly if a standard file were created containing the text, you would be able to edit it with **vi** or **ed**. Unfortunately, however, both of these editors are interactive in that they require you to direct their operation from the keyboard. What you want is to be able to specify **ed** type commands but on the command line to an editor and not in an interactive mode after the editor is running. This is precisely how the stream editor called **sed** is designed to be used. As the commands to **sed** are based on the equivalent commands to **ed** it should not be difficult to learn to use.

One thing you have to remember is that by its very nature sed is forced to edit lines as they fly by in transit as it were. This means that there is no point in trying to work out command sequences to **sed** that move backwards and forwards through the text out of sequence. It just cannot be done.

The default action of **sed** is to copy its standard input to its standard output one line at a time unchanged. If any editing commands are specified then in general a line will be read in, the commands applied to the line, and then the result written to the output. These actions are repeated until EOF. In the process of reading lines in, one other operation is performed that can be useful — the lines are counted. This allows you to specify a line number or range of lines to which the commands given will be applied. The lines not included in the range are just copied from input to output unchanged.

$ **cat /etc/passwd |sed's/:/ /g'**

This pipeline sends the contents of **/etc/passwd** into sed which then substitutes a space character for every occurrence of a colon on each line.

Note that no attempt is being made here to alter the contents of the password file. Only a copy is being taken and passed to **sed** which then sends its results to the standard output device. Notice also that the command string for **sed** is enclosed in quotes. This is to make sure that the shell does not alter any characters in the command string that are significant to the shell itself. Suppose you wanted to list just a few lines from a file you might try the following:

$ cat filename | sed '10,15p'

In **ed** this would print out just lines 10–15 and in **sed** it will do the same thing. But in **sed** the default action is also taking place at the same time so that what you actually get is a copy of the input file with duplicate copies of lines 10–15 embedded in there as well. What you really need is some way to suppress the default action so that only lines 10–15 appear as output. This can be done with the **−n** option which has no **ed** equivalent.

$ cat filename | sed −n '10, 15p'

Another command (**y**) for which there is no **ed** equivalent allows character transformation in much the same way as **tr** except that the character ranges of **tr** are not supported:

$ cat file1 | sed 'y/()/[]/' >file2

Here everything in the file file1 that is enclosed in round brackets will be changed so that it becomes enclosed in square brackets. The resulting lines of text are then written by I/O redirection into the file file2.

To delete lines using **sed** requires the **d** command:

$ sed '10, 15d'

removes lines 10–15 from its input just by failing to copy them across to the output. Very often you will not know the numbers of the lines upon which you wish to use a particular command. In these instances, as with **ed**, strings can be given between pairs of slash (**/**) characters. The strings will be used to determine which input lines will be selected for action.

$ sed '/^$/d'

will delete all blank lines from the input. Notice that unlike **ed** the search pattern is used on all lines of input, automatically looking for a match and hence a line upon which to perform the specified commands.

Finally, rather than specifying **sed** commands on the command line it is also possible to place them in a file and cause the file to be interpreted by using the **−f** option:

$ sed −f cmdfile

Here **sed** will run as usual but take its commands from the file cmdfile.

There are many more UNIX utilities which take their input from and send their output to the standard I/O devices and can therefore provide facilities which can be used to bolt together pipelines to perform all sorts of functions. In Chapter 6 you will see some examples of this while unravelling the power of shell programming.

5.8 COMMAND SUMMARY

cmp   Compares two files byte by byte and displays the byte and line number where they differ
cmp file 1 file 2

comm   Selects or rejects lines of text that are common to two previously sorted files
comm [− [1] [2] [3]] file1 file2

grep   Searches files for a given text string and prints out any lines that contain (do not contain −**v**) a match
grep [− [n] [v]] string file . . .

join   Joins together related lines in two previously sorted files. The output can be any selection of fields from joined lines
join [−0 field . . .] file1 file2

sed   Copies an input file to its output applying **ed** like edit commands in the process
sed [−f cmdfile] [editcmd] file . . .

sort   Sorts the lines of a text file into order. Several options available, including −**n** for sort in numeric order, −**f** to treat upper and lower case as the same thing, −**r** to reverse the order of sorting and −**t** to alter the field separator
sort [−option . . .] file . . .

tr   Copy standard input to standard output translating characters specified in the first parameter string for the corresponding characters in the second parameter string
tr string1 string2

Shell programming

Back in Chapter 3 you took an initial look at the standard UNIX shell and some of its facilities. These include controlling I/O redirection, setting up command pipelines, executing lists of commands contained in files (shell scripts) and shell variables. In that chapter I hinted that the shell was much more powerful than these ideas suggest and even provides facilities that would classify it as a programming language in its own right. Exploring these ideas in more detail is the subject of this chapter.

6.1 COMMANDS IN A LOOP

Suppose you have a file with contents like the following:

```
pc B302

jab B302

jwd B303

pjk B304

prb B304

mef B305

dm B305

dsh B306

mcw B306

jeg B307

eb B307
```

---

which essentially contains a list of names (or initials here) and room numbers. It is a simple matter to write a shell script that will print out a room number given a name:

grep $1 /usr/pc/roomfile

If this line is stored in the executable file **room** then a command like the following can be given:

$ room pjk
pjk B304

---

and the required output will be produced. Do not forget to use **chmod** to make your shell scripts executable. If now the following command is given:

$ room pjk jeg jab
pjk B304

---

then the output will be the same as before and not as you would like with a room number for each name.

The problem can be overcome by using a loop construct called **for**. This construct allows a group of commands to be repeated with different parameters each time round the loop. The general format of the shell **for** construct is:

for var in p1 p2 p3 ...
do
   command list
done

What happens is that a variable is declared (**var** in the format above) which is then given each of the values after the **in** keyword in turn. For each value that **var** holds, the command list between **do** and **done** is executed once.

Applying this to the room number example gives the new shell script:

```
for i in $*
do
        grep $i /usr/pc/roomfile
done
```

Now giving the previous command gives the required result:

$ room pjk jeg jab

pjk B304

jeg B307

jab B302

One small simplification is possible in this shell script. The **for** value list is so often **in $*** that this is the default if nothing is specified. This gives the final version of the shell script as:

```
for i
do
        grep $i /usr/pc/roomfile
done
```

Another similar example utilizes the contents of the standard system file **/etc/ttytype**. This file contains a list of terminal device names (tty01,tty02, etc.) and the system's best idea of what actual terminal type is connected to each device:

$ cat /etc/ttytype

```
tty06 vt52
tty07 vt100
tty08 adm3a
tty09 vt52
```

A simple shell program can tell you what actual terminal type is connected to each system terminal device or indeed vice versa.

Here is a version which given a list of terminal types will tell you the system devices that have terminals of the specified types connected to them:

```
for i
do
        echo $i terminals:
        grep $i /etc/ttytype | sed s/$i//
done
exit 0
```

If this script is given the name **ttys** then it can be run as follows:

$ **ttys vt52 vt100**
vt52 terminals:
tty06
tty09
vt100 terminals
tty07

The only thing that is not obvious about the operation of this shell script is the use of the:

exit 0

line at the end. Well, so far all the shell script examples have been rather lax. The standard system commands and shell scripts return a value at the end of their operation to specify whether or not their operation was successful. Any command that does terminate without error returns the value 0. This value is called the exit status of the command. Any non-zero exit status values indicate that an error occurred during program execution. As you may already have guessed, the **exit** command allows a shell script to return a given exit status.

6.2 TESTING THE EXIT STATUS

There is not really much point in having an exit status value from a command unless there is some way to test the value and perform one of several actions depending on the result.

The way to test the exit status in this manner is to use the shell's built-in **if–then–else** construct. The general form of this construct is:

if condition
then
   no error action
else
   error action
fi

Here, condition is the command whose exit status is being tested and the error and no error actions are lists of other commands to deal with each of the possibilities. A simple example takes a list of potential login names and tells you whether or not each of the names appears in the system password file.

```
for i
do
        if grep $i /etc/passwd >/dev/null 2>/dev/null
        then
                echo $i is a valid login name
        else
                echo $i is not a valid login name
        fi
done
exit 0
```

Notice that the **if–then–else** construct is terminated by the word **fi** which is just **if** spelled backwards. There are two other points to note about this shell script. First the condition command on the **if** line is a **grep** command that is being asked to find specified login names in the password file. Normally if any match is found then **grep** would print out the line where the match was found. In this application the print-out is not required, just the return of the exit status, so the **grep** standard output is redirected to a special place called **/dev/null**. Anything sent to **/dev/null** is just lost by the system never to be seen again. In this application it effectively forces any output from **grep** to be ignored as required. The last thing to notice is what looks like another output redirection on the end of the line.

2 > /dev/null

This **is** in fact another output redirection but not of standard I/O. As you will discover when you look at C later, a program not only has a standard input and a standard output channel (numbered 0 and 1) but it also has a standard place to send error messages (numbered 2) if any are generated. Error message output defaults to the screen so that even if standard output is redirected to a file, you will still see any error messages on your terminal.

In the example shell scripts, **grep** error output is not required either so it too is redirected, with:

2 >

to the system null device (**/dev/null**).

6.3 LOOPS WITH EXIT STATUS

The **for** loop you saw earlier does not enable you to test for an exit status; it only assigns a number of listed values in turn to a specified variable.

However, there are two loop constructs that will work with exit status values. The first is called **until** and in its general form it looks like:

until condition
do
   commands
done

This loop causes all commands between **do** and **done** to be executed repeatedly until the condition command returns a 'no error' exit status value (0). As an example:

```
until test -f $1
do
done
echo file $1 now exists
exit 0
```

The first thing to look at with this example is what the new command **test** does.

Most commands return an exit status as a side-effect of their operation. In the case of **test** its sole purpose is to return zero and non-zero exit status values depending on certain conditions specified as parameters. The most common **test** options are:

−d file	This returns a zero exit status if the specified file exists and is a directory
−f file	Returns a zero if 'file' exists and is just an ordinary file
−r file	Returns zero if 'file' exists and is readable
−w file	Returns zero if 'file' exists and is writable
−x file	Returns zero if 'file' exists and is executable
string	Returns zero if 'string' is not null, i.e. contains one or more characters
str1=str2	Returns zero if the two strings are identical

Going back to the example then:

test −f $1

is checking for the existence of the specified file. The **until** construct contains no commands between **do** and **done** so the construct will just loop round until **test** returns a zero value, when the file is found to exist. A message to this effect is printed when the loop ends. If the shell script is called **testfile** it can be executed as:

$ **testfile /usr/pc/datafile &**

Notice the ampersand (**&**) on the end of the line to force the command to run in the background. This needs to be done otherwise you would not get a shell prompt back until the file was found to exist — and it might be a long wait!

The other iterative construct for testing a command's exit status is the **while** loop:

while condition
do
    command
done

The action of the **while** construct is just the same as **until** except that the condition is reversed. The **until** construct loops until its condition is true (0). The **while** construct loops only while its condition is true (0) (i.e. until it is not true).

Here is an example that will check the **who** list every 30 seconds and sort out anyone who logged on or off since last looking.

```
>/tmp/old$$
while true
do
        who | sort >/tmp/new$$
        echo login:
        comm -23 /tmp/new$$ /tmp/old$$
        echo logout:
        comm -13 /tmp/new$$ /tmp/old$$
        mv /tmp/new$$ /tmp/old$$
        sleep 30
done
```

The first line of the script just creates a new and empty file in the system temporary file directory **/tmp**. The file name is composed of two parts, first the word **old**, then a number which is inserted by the shell instead of the **$$**. The actual number inserted is the UNIX process identity number for the shell you are running and as such it should be unique. This means that there should be no danger of overwriting some other user's temporary files.

The commands **true** and **false** just return a zero or non-zero exit status respectively so that the **while** construct in the example is just an infinite loop. Shell scripts for **true** and **false** are trivial:

```
# true
exit 0
```

and:

 # false
exit 1

Notice that preceding a line in a shell script with a hash (**#**) symbol makes the line a comment.

The body of the **while** loop in the example is quite straightforward and is left for you to sort out as an exercise. The only line to explain is:

sleep 30

and this just causes the program to pause in its execution for the specified length of time in seconds. Once again as the script is an infinite loop it is a good idea to run it in the background if you want your shell prompt back.

6.4 MULTIPLE BRANCH CONSTRUCT

Now you have seen the way to perform loops and conditional statements under the control of a commands exit status. You have also seen how to loop under the control of a shell variable value. What you have not yet seen is how to perform a multiway branch depending on a shell variable value. This is done with a **case** statement:

```
case $var in
   string1)
     commands1;;
   string2)
     commands2;;
   *)
     default commands;;
esac
```

What happens here is that the value of the control variable (var) is compared with each of the test string values (string1, string2, etc.) in turn looking for a match. If a match is found then the commands associated with that test string value will be executed. Each set of commands is terminated with a double semicolon (;;). If no other match is found then eventually the asterisk (*) will be reached and it is arranged that this is always a match for any value that the variable may hold. The asterisk's commands therefore form the default action of the **case** construct. Notice that **case** ends with **esac** (which is just case spelled backwards).

As an example look at the following shell script called **append** which can take either one or two parameters. If only one parameter is given then it is the name of an existing file to which will be appended any text entered from the keyboard until end of file. If a second parameter is given then it too should be the name of a file which will be used as the source of the text to append to the first file specified. This is instead of using text from the keyboard:

```
case $# in
        1) cat >>$1;;
        2) cat >>$1 <$2;;
        *) echo "usage: append tofile [fromfile]";;
esac
exit 0
```

The **$#** variable contains the number of positional parameters on the command line excluding the command name itself. For the **append** command this value should either be one or two depending upon whether one file name or two file names appear on the command line as parameters. An appropriate error message is printed if **$#** is not one or two as required.

6.5 INTERACTIVE INPUT

Sometimes you may want to take input from the keyboard to be assigned to a shell variable while a shell script is running. This can be done with the **read** command:

```
while true
do
        read word
        case $word in
                end) exit 0;;
                *) echo $word;;
        esac
done
```

This program just takes any words typed at the keyboard and echoes them to the screen until the word **end** is entered. The program then terminates with a 0 exit status. The resultant text from a program can also be assigned to a shell variable. It is done just by enclosing the command between a pair of reverse apostrophes:

mypath=‘pwd‘

Here the **pwd** command will be executed. Normally it would print the path to the current working directory. But enclosed between reverse apostrophes this information is just returned as a result to be assigned in this example to the shell variable **mypath**.

6.6 SIGNALS

As you already know, you can stop a running program by sending an interrupt signal from the keyboard (usually DEL or ctrl–c). Another way to achieve a similar effect is to press ctrl–\. The ctrl–\ sequence is called a quit signal. It is also possible in certain circumstances for another piece of software to send a message called a terminate signal to your program and this will also cause it to stop. These are just three examples of a whole lot of signal conditions that can be received by your programs. (You will see more details about signals in Section 14.9.) However, the default action taken by your program when it receives a signal is to terminate execution. This is just one of three types of action that can be taken by a shell script when a signal is received. Another possibility is that the signal can be ignored and the third action is that a command sequence can be executed.

Each signal in the system is given a numerical value. The three you have seen are:

interrupt   2
quit   3
terminate   15

The actions taken on receipt of these signals can be changed with the **trap** command.

A **trap** instruction followed by the value of a signal is the sequence to restore the default (terminate) action of that signal.

---

trap 2
 # sets interrupt to default action
trap 3 15
 # sets quit and terminate to default action

Executing a command or sequence of commands on receipt of a signal can be done as follows:

trap "commands" 2 3

When either of the interrupt or quit signals is received, the above line will cause execution of the commands within the quotes. For example, if you have opened a temporary file in **/tmp**, you really should make sure that it gets deleted if at all possible. The following line of code will make sure that a temporary file called **tmpfile** is deleted from **/tmp** if an interrupt or quit signal is received from the keyboard:

trap "rm /tmp/tmpfile ; exit 0" 2 3

Notice the semicolon which is used to separate commands on the same line.

This is why **case** selections end with a double semicolon to distinguish one from the other.

Finally, ignoring a signal uses the same idea as above but with a null command string:

trap "" 2 3 15

6.7 SUMMARY

6.7.1 Commands

false	Command to return a non-zero exit status. **false**
sleep	Suspends program execution for a specified number of seconds. **sleep time**
test	Test for a condition specified by command line option. Options include: **−r** test if file readable, **−w** test if file writable, **−x** test if file executable/searchable, **−d** test for a directory, **−f** test for an ordinary file, etc. Test can also compare strings. **test [− option . . .]** **test string1 = string2**
true	Command to return a zero exit status. **true**

6.7.2 Shell features

#	Add comments to shell scripts
2 >	Redirect error output
$$	Returns process id for current shell
'cmd'	Return **cmd** output as a string
case	String value selection statement
exit	Terminate program with given status
for	String value iteration statement
if	Boolean value selection statement
read	Take input variable values
trap	Control the treatment of signals
until	Boolean value iteration statement
while	Boolean value iteration statement

The C programming language

C program structure | 7

So far, you have spent six chapters studying the facilities provided by the UNIX operating system and its many standard commands. What you may not have realized or even thought about is that all this software has been written in the high-level programming language C. And it is to this topic that Part Two of the book is devoted.

7.1 FUNCTIONS

Any C program is made up of one or more blocks of program code that are called functions. Each function in a C program has the following general format:

```
type name (parameter list)
parameter declarations
{
      function body;
}
```

In its most complex form a function can have values passed to it when it is called, as data for it to work on. A function can also return a value as the result of its operation. These aspects of functions will be covered later, but for now a simpler function format will suffice:

```
name ()
{
      function body;
}
```

This shows that a function consists of two main parts. Firstly, its name — this can be any combination of upper- and lower-case letters, digits and the underscore character, but must not begin with a digit. For example:

```
x
VAR1
time_of_day
```

are all valid function names. Whereas:

ØPEN
day—of—week

are invalid, the first because it starts with a digit, the second because it contains an invalid character, the minus sign (−). Every function must have a name and you have complete freedom to choose whatever names you wish. But you should remember that some versions of C will only look at the first eight characters of the name. So the two names:

Days _ of _ week
Days _ of _ month

will not be recognized as two unique names but will be treated as the same name because they do not differ in the first eight characters.

The second main part of a function is the function body. This is the part of the function that consists of the individual statements that perform the actions of the function. As you will see, the function body can consist of any number of lines of code which are of two basic types, but for the sake of readability the length is best kept below about 50 lines.

The two basic types of lines in the function body are either expressions followed by a semicolon (;) or lines to control the flow of execution around the program. Both of these types of lines are important enough to have complete chapters devoted to them. Expressions are dealt with in Chapter 8 and flow control constructs in Chapter 10.

7.2 THE FIRST PROGRAM

The standard 'first C program' that everyone uses is one which will print the immortal words "Hello, world" on to the terminal screen:

```
first()
{
        printf("Hello, world\n");
}
```

As you can see, the above lines conform to the simplified function format given previously, where the name of the function is first and the function body is the single line

printf("Hello, world\n");

The fact that the function body line is an expression line can be seen by the fact that it is terminated with a semicolon. In C a function can be called just by using its name. This is followed by a pair of round brackets containing any information that needs to be passed to the function. You can see from this that the use of the word **printf** in the above function body is an example of a call to a function named **printf**. The brackets following the **printf** call contain the string **"Hello, world\n"** which is the information that is passed as a parameter to the **printf** function for it to work on. **printf** is a function just like any that you may write for yourself except that it has already been compiled, along with a lot of other standard functions, into a library that will automatically be linked into your own programs when they are compiled. This means that you do not have to provide any code for **printf**, it is just called from the standard library.

There is nothing magical about the standard function library — it just contains ordinary functions that you might have written for yourself. As such it does mean that the standard library is not strictly part of the C language, indeed you can replace it with your own functions if the need arises.

In its simplest form, a call to the **printf** function just prints out the contents of its parameter string to the standard output device (which is your terminal screen unless output has been redirected). The characters backslash followed by 'n' **(\n)** on the end of the parameter string **"Hello, world\n"** are treated by the C compiler as a single newline character, returning the terminal cursor to the start of the next line on the screen.

7.3 COMPILING PROGRAMS

If you have entered the example program into an editor then save it under the name **first.c**. It is most important that any C program files you create should have names that end with the suffix **.c** so that the C compiler will recognize them.

You can compile the contents of the file **first.c** with the command line:

$ **cc first.c**

cc is the command name for the C compiler and this is followed by the full name (including the .c) of the file to be compiled.

When you enter this command you will in fact get an error message something like:

Undefined symbol "main"

This is a report that says that a function called **main** was expected but was not found. Why is this? Well consider: if a program consists of several functions, what will determine which of them is executed first at run time and will thus be in control of the rest? One possibility would be to use the first function declared in the file but because a C program can be split up over several files, the choice is not made this way. Instead, of all the possible names that can be used for functions one special name is selected and used automatically by the compiler. That special name is **main** and it means that every C program must have somewhere within it a function called **main**. It need not be the first function in the program or even in the first file of a multiple file program, but it must appear somewhere in every C program.

The solution to the error message then is simple — add a function called **main** to the file **first.c** as follows:

```
main()
{
        first();
}


first()
{
        printf("Hello, world\n");
}
```

The program now consists of two functions, **main** and **first**. Execution of the program will begin at the start of the function body of **main**. All this does is to call the function **first** whose operation you have already studied. Notice that even though the function **first** requires no parameter values to be passed to it, the brackets are still required after the call to **first** in the body of **main**.

This example shows that the procedure for calling your own functions is just the same as calling standard library functions.

Assuming that your program is still called **first.c** then the command line:

$ cc first.c

should not produce any errors this time. If it does, then check carefully that you have typed everything in exactly as shown, especially the different sorts of brackets and the positions of the semicolons.

In this particular example it is not actually necessary to use two different functions, **first** and **main**. Only one of them is needed and since every program must contain a function called **main**, this is the one to choose:

```
main()
{
        printf("Hello, world\n");
}
```

When you can get this example program to compile without error take a look at the contents of the directory you have been working in:

$ ls —L

```
-rwx------  1 pc      pc      8192 Jul 18 12:33 a.out
-rw-------  1 pc      pc        39 Jul 18 12:32 first.c
```

What you see here is the source file (i.e. the file containing the C code) **first.c** and a new file called **a.out** that has been produced by the compiler. Notice that this new file is flagged as executable. In fact this file is the executable ouput produced by the compiler from your source code. The name **a.out** is just the default name used when you supplied no alternative name.

To execute the program all you have to do is to specify its name just like any other command program:

```
$ a.out
```

Hello, world

---

and the program produces the output **"Hello, world"** just as expected. It is possible to rename the file **a.out** with the **mv** command as you have already seen or it is possible to get the compiler to assign the required name to its output to start with. This is done with the **−o** parameter to the **cc** command as follows:

```
$ cc first.c −o first
```

Notice that the space between the **−o** and the file name **first** is needed. The output from the compiler will now be called **first** and this is the command name to use when executing the program.

Going back to the listings of the **"Hello, world"** programs, you can see a particular textual layout depicted in these listings. It is a good idea to use some sort of indentation in your own programs to highlight the structure of the code. The actual indentation style, however, is left very much to the individual — the C compiler does not impose any particular structural layout and indeed may even be looked upon as perhaps too lenient in this respect. It is most important that you should develop some kind of programming style which above all should be consistent; you will find it such a help when trying to read or debug your code later.

Before progressing to Chapter 8, try changing the layout of the example programs as a start to finding a style to suit you and to convince yourself that different styles do not alter the meaning of the program to the compiler. After you have done this try altering the programs in various ways including the introduction of errors to see what effects the changes have on the compiled code or what error messages are produced by the compiler.

This last is a particularly useful exercise as it will allow you to see what sorts of errors to look for in your programs when particular error messages are generated during compilation runs on larger programs.

8	# C basics

8.1 VALUE TYPES

A variable in a C program needs to be thought of as a place in the computer's memory that can be used to store a value. In C these values can be of several different types, the most common being **char**, **int**, **float** and **double**.

8.1.1 char

The specification for C does not give any hard and fast rules about the sizes of the different value types. But in general, values of type **char** are 8 bits wide which means that a **char** value can be any single ASCII or EBCDIC character. Obviously, an 8-bit **char** can have one of 256 different values, but again C does not specify whether these values should be signed (-128 to $+127$) or unsigned ($0-255$) so care must be taken as you will see, when the code needs to be portable.

8.1.2 int

This is short for integer, meaning whole number. Again no fixed size is specified, though values of type **int** are signed quantities usually either 16 bits or 32 bits wide. This gives **int** values a numeric range of either $-32\,768$ to $+32\,767$ (16 bit) or $-2\,147\,483\,648$ to $+2\,147\,483\,647$ (32 bit).

8.1.3 float

Values of type **float** have two parts; the first is an integer part up to the decimal point and the second is the fractional part after the decimal point. Depending on the format in which these values are stored, lots of different ranges are possible. A typical implementation might store **float** values in 32 bits and give a range $-1E38$ to $+1E38$ ($1E38$ is scientific notation meaning a 1 followed by 38 zeros). This may seem to be a much greater range than was possible with **int** values of the same 32-bit size but there is a trade-off. What **floats** gain in numeric range, they lose in the precision of the stored values. The typical 32-bit **float** implementation will only have a numeric precision of 6 or 7 digits while **ints** of the same size have a precision of 9 or 10 digits. This means that a value like 1 234 567 890.0 will only be stored as 1 234 567 000.0 after the loss of precision.

8.1.4 double

To overcome some of the problem of the loss of precision in **float** values **double** values are also supported. Typically **double** values would take twice the storage space of **floats** (i.e. up to 64 bits) but would allow a precision of 16 or 17 significant digits. Obviously, dealing with numbers this big requires a lot more storage space than the other value types.

8.1.5 Modified types

In order to try to give you more control over the sizes and types of data values, C also supports some modified forms of the **char** and **int** types.

The type modifiers use the keywords **short, long** and **unsigned**. All three of these can be applied to **int** values to give:

short int usually stored in 16 bits
long int usually stored in 32 bits
unsigned int; this is the same size as **int** but all the values are positive so that the ranges become 0–65 535 (if **int** is 16 bit) or 0–4 294 967 295 (for 32 bit)

To avoid the difficulty of deciding whether **chars** are signed or unsigned it is also acceptable to specify:

unsigned char, which fixes the range of **char** values as 0–255

8.2 VARIABLES

You have seen that values can be of several different types. In C, variables are areas of memory that are set aside to hold values. Each such area of memory is given a name that can be used to refer to the value that is stored there. A variable name must begin with either a letter or an underscore (_) character. This may then optionally be followed by one or more further letters, under-scores or digits. In most cases, the C compiler will only look at the first eight characters of a variable name so that these characters need to be unique in any situation where confusion might arise.

In order for the compiler to work out how much space to set aside for each variable in your programs, it needs to be told what type of value each variable is to hold. Telling the compiler the type of value to associate with each variable name is done at the same time as declaring the names of the variables themselves. A declaration line consists of a value type specification followed by a list of variable names whose memory locations will hold values of the type specified:

int flag,count;

float rain_fall,temperature;

These two lines declare the variable names **flag** and **count** which will be associated with memory areas holding values of type **int** and the variable names **rain_fall** and **temperature** which will hold values of type **float**.

Notice that in the list of variable names, the names are separated by commas and that the last name is followed by a semicolon. The semicolon is required even if only one variable name is declared on a line. The declarations for each of the different types may be given in any order and in any quantity so that the same four variables may also have been declared as:

float temperature;

int count,flag;

float rain_fall;

8.3 CONSTANTS

Values in a program which will not change are usually specified as constants rather than being assigned to a variable. The three main types of constants are numeric, character and string as follows.

8.3.1 Numeric constants

Ordinary decimal integer values are specified just by giving the value (e.g. 123). Sometimes, if **long** is stored in more bits than **int**, it is desirable to specify a **long int** constant even though the value may be small enough to fit in an ordinary **int** space. This is done by following the constant value with the letter **L** (or **l**) so that 123L would be the constant value 123 but represented as a **long int**. As well as decimal values, integer constants can also be specified either in the octal number base by preceding the value with a zero (123 decimal is equivalent to 0173 octal) or in hexadecimal by preceding the value with a zero followed by the letter **X** or **x** (123 decimal is equivalent to 0x7b hexadecimal).

Finally, numeric constants can also be of type **float** in one of two different formats: either as two integers separated by a full stop (123.0 or 12.672, etc.) or in scientific notation using the exponent operator (E). For example, 123.0 may be represented as 1.23E2 (i.e. 1.23 times 10 to the power 2) or as 12.3E1 (i.e. 12.3 times 10) or even 0.000123E6 (i.e. 0.000123 times 10 to the power 6).

8.3.2 Character constants

As you have seen, values of type **char** are normally 8 bits wide, giving them a range of -128 to $+127$ for signed values or $0-255$ for unsigned values. However, as their name implies, **char** variables are most often used to store single character values from the machine's underlying character set. Unfortunately, there are two very common standards for representing characters. One is called ASCII (American Standard Code for Information Interchange) and the other is called EBCDIC (Extended Binary Coded Decimal Interchange Code). The problem with having two codes is that all the letters, numbers and special characters have different numeric representations in the two codes. For example:

Character	ASCII code	EBCDIC code
A	65	193
1	49	241
+	43	78

This means that to assign the value representing a particular character to a **char** variable you need to know which code is in use and that is hardly portable. To overcome this problem, C allows a character constant to be specified as a character enclosed in single quote marks (") which the compiler will then translate to a value in the correct code:

Character constant	ASCII code	EBCDIC code
'A'	65	193
'1'	49	241
'+'	43	78

Sometimes it may happen that the character you want to represent may not be a printable character, such as backspace or newline, or the character may have some special meaning to C and cannot be enclosed in single quotes directly such as the single quote itself, for example. In this case special escape sequences are used to represent these characters:

Escape sequence	Character
'\n'	Newline (LF)
'\r'	Carriage return (CR)
'\t'	Horizontal tab (HT)
'\b'	Backspace (BS)
'\''	Single quote
'\"'	Double quote
'\\'	Backslash

Notice that in each case the two-character sequence consisting of the backslash character (\) and the following character are treated together as a single **char** value in the appropriate character code.

For some special applications even the provision of the escape sequences may not be sufficient. For these applications it is possible to specify any **char**-sized value by the backslash character followed by one to three octal digits giving the required characters numeric value in the appropriate code.

Character constant	ASCII equivalent
'\14'	Form feed (FF)
'\7'	BELL
'\0'	NULL

8.3.3 String constants

A string in this context means a string of characters or **char** values. String constants are stored in memory as a set of **char** values in consecutive memory locations. The string itself should be enclosed in double quotes rather than single quotes and may contain any sequence of character constants including escape sequence characters. When a string is stored in memory the C compiler automatically appends a '\0' character on the end which acts as the termination character.

String	Notes
"ABCDEF"	This is a string occupying seven consecutive memory locations, six for letters A–F and one for '\0' appended to the end
"Hello\n"	This is also seven characters long. 'H', 'e', 'l', 'l', 'o' is five, '\n' is one and '\0' is the last

8.4 EXPRESSIONS

Expressions in C are the action statements of the language and as such deserve fairly close scrutiny. An expression is a collection of one or more operands interspersed with zero or more operators. You have already seen most of the things that qualify for the title of operand. These include variable values, the results of function calls and character, string or numeric constants.

8.4.1 Operators

The list of operators in C is somewhat larger than the list of operand types and they can be split into several convenient groups for study purposes.

(a) Arithmetic operators

This is the name given to the standard add, subtract, multiply and divide operators. These are called binary operators as they all work on two operands and they are written and used as follows:

Operator	Symbol	Example	Meaning
Add	+	**a + 7**	Adds 7 to the value of variable **a**
Subtract	−	**b − c**	Subtracts the value of **c** from the value of **b**
Multiply	*	**f * 7.9**	Multiply the value of **f** by the float constant 7.9
Divide	/	**7 / 3**	Divide the value 7 by the value 3

Notice that in this last example the two operands in the division (7 and 3) are both integers. In this case the result of the division will be rounded so that it too is an integer value. In order to produce a **float** result in a case like this it is necessary to use at least one float operand:

7.0/3   This will give the **float** result 2.3333, etc.

The other arithmetic operators in C are:

Operator	Symbol	Example	Meaning
Modulus	%	**7 % 3**	Gives the remainder on integer division. 7/3 is 2 remainder 1, so 7%3 is 1
Minus	−	**−1**	This is called a unary operator because it operates on one operand. Minus changes the sign of its operand

(b) Comparison operators

There are six binary operators in this section each of which returns a value of either 0 or 1 depending on the truth or otherwise of the expression. Note that in C any expression with value 0 can be used as a boolean FALSE value in a comparison, and any non-zero value represents boolean TRUE.

The six operators are:

==	Equal to
!=	Not equal to
<	Less than
>	Greater than
<=	Less than or equal to
>=	Greater than or equal to

If **x** has the value 6 and **y** has the value 7 then the following comparison expressions give the boolean results shown:

Expression	Boolean result	Notes
x == 6	1	TRUE — **x** is equal to **6**
y != x	1	TRUE — **y** is not equal to **x**
y < x	0	FALSE — **y** is not less than **x**
y > x	1	TRUE — **y** is greater than **x**
y <= 2	0	FALSE — **y** not less than or equal to **2**
y >= 7	1	TRUE — **y** is greater than or equal to **7**

(c) Logical operators

Sometimes it is useful to be able to generate a compound conditional expression consisting of two or more comparison expressions concatenated together. This facility is provided by two binary logical operators **&&** (AND) and ‖ (inclusive OR). For example:

```
x==6 && y==7
```

This whole expression will be TRUE (i.e. return the value 1) if both x equals 6 AND y equals 7, and FALSE (0) otherwise.

```
x< 5 ‖ x > 8
```

This whole expression will be TRUE (1) if either x is less than 5 OR x is greater than 8 and FALSE (0) otherwise.

In general in C no evaluation order is imposed on the compiler when evaluating the left and right operands of a binary operator. This is to give the potential for improvements in efficiency in the generated code. However, for the binary logical operators an order of operand evaluation is specified. It should always be done left operand first. After this it may still be necessary to evaluate the right operand but sometimes not. For example:

AND (&&)

Left operand value	Right operand value	Result value
Zero	Not evaluated	0
Non-zero	Zero	0
Non-zero	Non-zero	1

---

and:

OR (||)

Left operand value	Right operand value	Result value
Zero	Zero	0
Zero	Non-zero	1
Non-zero	Not evaluated	1

Remember that in comparison and logical operator evaluation any zero-valued operand represents FALSE and any non-zero-valued operand represents TRUE. This means that the following expressions are also valid and have the values shown:

Expression	Value
6||7	1
6||0	1
6&&7	1
0&&7	0

Notice in the first two expressions with the || (**OR**) operator the rules show that the right operand is not evaluated. This makes sense as you can confirm for yourself that it does not matter whether the right operand is zero or non-zero, with a non-zero (TRUE) left operand the result will always be 1 (TRUE).

A similar line of reasoning shows that if the left operand of an **&&** (**AND**) operator has a zero value then there is no point in evaluating the right operand as its value cannot affect the result — it will always be zero. Also in with the logical operators is a unary operator called **NOT** and given the exclamation mark (!) as its symbol.

The **NOT** operator inverts the logical sense of its single operand, converting **TRUE** values to **FALSE** and **FALSE** values to **TRUE**. For example:

Expression	Value	Notes
!7	0	7 is **TRUE** so becomes **FALSE** (zero)
!0	1	0 is **FALSE** so becomes **TRUE** (non-zero)

(d) Bitwise operators

The bitwise operators operate only on character and integer values. To understand their operation you need to translate their operand values into binary numbers, i.e. a sequence of bits that each have values either of 0 or 1. Once you have the binary representation of the operand values, the bitwise operators then perform action on these individual bits.

In total there are five binary bitwise operators and one unary bitwise operator. They are:

Operator	Operation
&	**AND** (binary)
|	**OR** (binary)
^	**XOR** (binary)
<<	**Left shift** (binary)
>>	**Right shift** (binary)
~	1's complement (unary)

And they operate as follows.

AND (&)

In order to work out the result of applying the bitwise **AND** operator to the binary representation of its two operands the following truth table should be applied to corresponding pairs of bits in the two operands to give the bits of the result.

Left operand bit	Right operand bit	Result bit
0	0	0
0	1	0
1	0	0
1	1	1

For example:

26 & 11

in binary becomes (8-bit **chars**):

00011010 & 00001011

applying the truth table to corresponding bits:

00011010 left operand

00001011 right operand

00001010 result (in decimal = 10)

OR (|)

The **OR** operator's operation is similar to that of the **AND** operator except that a different truth table is used:

Left operand bit	Right operand bit	Result bit
0	0	0
0	1	1
1	0	1
1	1	1

For example:

41 | 39

in binary becomes (8-bit chars)

00101001 | 00100111

applying the truth table to corresponding bits:

00101001 left operand

00100111 right operand

00101111 result (in decimal = 47)

The most common use for the bitwise **AND** and **OR** operators is in bit masking. This is a technique most often used for setting to 1 or resetting to 0 an individual bit or several bits within a character or integer value.

As you have seen, the **AND** operator puts a 1 bit in the result in every bit position where there is a 1 bit in both of the operand values. The **OR** operator puts a 1 bit in the result in every bit position where there is a 1 bit in either of the operand values.

To take a bit-masking example, if you want to set bit 4 in a character value to 1 without affecting the rest of the value, you would use the **OR** operator to bitwise **OR** the value with a number that has just bit 4 set to 1. The decimal value of the binary number with just bit 4 set is 16. So the expression:

byte | 16

would give as a result the value of the variable byte with bit 4 set to 1.

Suppose byte initially contained the value 164 then the expression would give:

```
byte=164=10100100
     16=00010000
 result=10110100=180
```

As you can see, bit 4 which was originally 0 is set to 1 in the result while the rest of the bits remain unchanged.

In general to set any specific pattern of bits in a value, you need to **OR** the value with the number that has just the required bit or bits set. Conversely, to reset given bits in a value to 0 you need to **AND** the value with the number that has just the required bit or bits reset to 0 and the other bits set to 1. For example, taking the previous result of 180, if you wanted to reset bit 5 you would need to **AND** 180 with the value 223 as follows:

180 = 10110100

223 = 11011111 Just bit 5 reset

result=10010100=148

As you can see, performing the **AND** operator with 223 just resets bit 5 in the result without affecting the rest of the value as required.

XOR (^)

This is the third binary bitwise operator, and it operates in just the same way as **AND** and **OR** except that a different truth table is used:

Left operand bit	Right operand bit	Result bits
0	0	0
0	1	1
1	0	1
1	1	0

For example:

150 ^ 165

in binary becomes (8-bit chars):

10010110 ^ 10100101

applying the truth table to corresponding bits

10010110 left operand

10100101 right operand

00110011 result (in decimal = 51)

Notice the result only has 1 bits in positions where the two corresponding bits from the operands were not the same as each other.

(e) Shift operators

The action of the two shift operators is also best described by translating the value of their left operands into binary. What the shift operators do is to allow the entire bit pattern of the left operand to be left or right shifted by the number of bit positions specified by the right operand. For example:

113 > > 3

will take the binary pattern for the value 113 and right shift it 3 bit positions:

113=01110001

so

01110001 > > 3

gives

00001110

Notice when the right shift operation takes place that any bits shifted off are lost. Also notice that zero bits are shifted into the left-hand end of the number to take up the gaps left by the bits lost from the right-hand end.

The left shift operator (<<) operates exactly the same way as the right shift but in the opposite direction. For example:

31 < < 2

in binary

31 = 00011111

so

00011111 < < 2

gives

01111100

The unary member of the bitwise operator set is the 1's complement operator. This operator has a single operand and what the operator does is to invert the values of all the bits in the binary representation of the operand value. That is, it translates all the 1 bits into 0s and all the 0 bits into 1s.

As an 8-bit value ˜12 gives 243, as follows:

12 = 00001100

˜12 = 11110011 = 243

(f) Assignment operators

Unlike most other languages, assigning the value of an expression to a variable in C is performed by a true binary operator. This means that assignment may be used just like any other operator in an expression, and just like all the other operators a value is generated that can be used elsewhere. In fact, the value generated by an assignment operator is the value that is assigned to its left-hand operand. For example:

k=7	Assigns the value 7 to the variable k. As 7 is the value assigned to k, this is the value of the whole expression
j=(k=7)	Here 7 is still assigned to k in the brackets. The value 7 is also returned from the bracketed expression and assigned to j

The operand on the left of an assignment operator has to be either a variable or at least some other expression that ends up pointing to a location of memory in which the right-hand expression value may be stored. Such a left-hand expression value is called an lvalue.

The simple equals sign is not the only assignment operator in C, there are several more. Very often in programming there is a need for expressions like:

a = a + 10

b = b * 6

c = c & 0x0f

where the value of a variable is modified in some way and then the value is reassigned to the same variable. In C there is a shorthand way of expressing this type of assignment for quite a few binary operators:

Standard expression	Shorthand expressions
a = a + 10	a += 10
b = b * 6	b *= 6
c = c & 0x0f	c &= 0x0f

Notice that in the shorthand version the symbol pairs +=, *= and &= represent single operators. The full list of operators that can be used in this way are:

+=	Addition
−=	Subtraction
*=	Multiplication
/=	Division (integer or real)
%=	Modulus (remainder on integer division)
&=	Bitwise **AND**
|=	Bitwise **OR**

^ =	Bitwise **XOR**
< <=	Bitwise left shift
> >=	Bitwise right shift

■ Half-time test!

There are few languages that would not have run out of operators by now — C, however, still has quite a few left. Before going on to look at them though, have a look at these few questions just to consolidate what you have seen so far.

What value is assigned to the variable x in each of the following cases?

(a) x = 8 / 3
(b) x = 8 % 3
(c) x = 8 != 3
(d) x = 8 <= 3
(e) x = 8 && 3
(f) x = 8 & 3
(g) x = 8 << 3
(h) x = 8 ^ 3
(i) x = 8 | 3
(j) x = 8 >> 3

Try to tackle all the questions before looking at the answers.

(a) 2
(b) 2
(c) 1
(d) 0
(e) 1
(f) 0
(g) 64
(h) 11
(i) 11
(j) 1

If you got them all right then press on. Otherwise you may find some revision useful. □

(g) Increment/decrement operators

It often happens that you will want to increment or decrement the value of a variable by 1. This can be done as follows:

x = x + 1

or

x += 1

as you have already seen. Another special notation that can be used with the same effect is:

x++

or

++x

The equivalent for decrement would be:

x--

or

--x

The increment (++) and decrement (--) operators can be used either before (as a prefix) or after (as a postfix) the variable that they are to operate on. In the simple case where the expression only increments or decrements a variable it does not make any difference whether the prefix or postfix version is used. However, when the increment or decrement forms part of a more complex expression, there is a difference not to the variable operated on but to the value presented by this term to the rest of the expression. If a prefix operator is used then the increment/decrement will be performed on the variable before the variable value is used in the rest of the expression. If a postfix operator is used then the increment/decrement is performed on the variable after the variable value is used.

For example, assume the variable k has been declared to be an **int** and has been assigned a value of 7:

Expression text	k value used in evaluation	k value after evaluation	Expression value
++k + 3	8	8	11
--k + 3	6	6	9
3 + k++	7	8	10
3 + k--	7	6	10

(h) Conditional operator

The use of the conditional operator allows an expression to return one of two different values depending on the result of a condition that is evaluated first.

Conditional expressions use the operator symbols question mark (?) and colon (:) in the following way:

(x > 7) ? 2 : 3

What this says is that if x is greater than 7 then the expression value is 2, otherwise the expression value is 3.

In general, the format for a conditional expression is:

a ? b : c

where a, b and c can be any C expressions.

Evaluation of this expression begins with the evaluation of the sub-expression a. If the value of a is TRUE (i.e. non-zero) then the whole conditional expression evaluates to the value of the sub-expression b. If the value of a is FALSE (i.e. zero) then the conditional expression returns the value of the sub-expression c.

A conditional expression can be used anywhere that an ordinary expression would be acceptable.

(i) Comma operator

As you will see in Section 10.3, there are places in C programs where the syntax rules allow the insertion of a single expression to give a value to one of the flow control constructs. Sometimes it will happen that you may wish to place two or more separate expressions in the space that C has reserved for one. This can be done using the comma operator:

j++, k+7

The comma operator does not combine the values of the two expressions (j++ and k+7) in any way — they are evaluated as two completely separate expressions. The overall value of a set of sub-expressions connected together by the comma operator is the value of the rightmost sub-expression. In the example above the variable j would be post-incremented by 1 and then the expression k+7 would be evaluated using the current value of k. As k+7 is the rightmost sub-expression in the example then this is the value returned by the overall expression. With the comma operator, the individual sub-expressions are always evaluated left to right.

(j) Type conversion operator

There are situations where an operand in an expression may be of a particular data type and you would like to change it to another type. Suppose for example that you have declared two variables (x and y say) to be of type **int**. Evaluating the expression:

x/y

will assume the use of integer division and truncate the result to an integer value. This may not be what you intended. To overcome the problem, C provides a method for converting the values of operands (though not the operands themselves) from one type to another. All that you do is to precede the operand whose value is to be type changed by the required type enclosed in round brackets:

(float)x / (float)y

This expression is now evaluated by taking the value of x and translating it to a **float** value and then taking the value of y and translating it to **float**. The two resulting **float** values are then divided as required using floating point division to give a floating point result.

The type conversion operator (enclosing a type in brackets) is a unary operator called a **cast**.

(k) The sizeof operator

Different C implementations can use different amounts of memory for storing basic data types as you have already seen. In situations where you need to incorporate the size of some object into an expression but you also need the code to be portable across different machines the **sizeof** unary operator comes to the rescue. The **sizeof** operator computes the size of any object at compile time. The expression:

sizeof (object)

returns an integer value equal to the size in bytes of the specified object (in general a byte is the same size as a char — 8 bits). The object itself can be the name of any sort of variable or the name of a basic type (like **int** or **float**, etc.).

(l) Other operators

There are still five operators left to look at but these will be explained in later chapters. Two are * and & used as unary operators, and a third is a binary operator []. These will be covered in Chapter 11 on pointers and arrays. The other two are $->$ and dot (.) which are dealt with in Chapter 13 on structures and unions.

8.5 EXPRESSION EVALUATION

You have already seen that, except in the cases of &&, || and comma (,), the order in which the operands of any particular operator are evaluated is unspecified. However, the same thing is not true of the operators themselves. In this case there is a definite order of evaluation based on a few simple rules. The first rule is that each operator is given a priority level or precedence and that the operators in any single expression are evaluated starting with the highest precedence operators and working through to the lowest precedence operators. Table 8.1 shows that there are 44 operators in total split into 15 different precedence groups, with the highest precedence operators at the top. The second rule specifies which operator to evaluate first if two or more operators of the same precedence are encountered in the same expression. This is done by giving each of the 15 precedence groups an associativity value which specifies whether the equal precedence operators should be evaluated from left to right or from right to left. The associativity column in Table 8.1 gives this information for each precedence group.

You have seen that a C expression is any syntactically correct combination of these operators and their operands. An executable statement in C is just any valid expression followed by a semicolon.

8.5.1 Automatic type conversions

The operands of binary operators need to be of compatible types. When operands of different types are encountered they are generally converted automatically to the same type according to simple rules. First, **char** and **short** values are converted to **int** which allows these integer types to be used interchangeably. Then for arithmetic operators **float** values are converted to **double**. Then when an arithmetic operator is evaluated, if the two operands are still of different types, the lower type operand value is converted to the type of the higher operand value in the following table:

higher	double
	long
	unsigned
lower	int

The operator is then evaluated with both operands of the higher type and the result is also of the higher type. For the assignment operators there is a further rule that the type of the expression evaluated on the right-hand side is

Table 8.1

Symbol	Name	Operator associativity	Operand evaluation
() [] −> .	Parenthesis Array element Structure pointer Structure member	L–R	Unspecified
! ~ ++ −− − (type) * & sizeof	Logical NOT Bitwise NOT Increment Decrement Minus Cast Contents of Address of Object size	R–L ALL UNARY	Unspecified
* / %	Multiply Divide Modulus	L–R	Unspecified
+ −	Add Subtract	L–R	Unspecified
<< >>	Left shift Right shift	L–R	Unspecified
< > <= >=	Less than Greater than Less than or equal to Greater than or equal to	L–R	Unspecified
== !=	Equal to Not equal to	L–R	Unspecified
&	Bitwise AND	L–R	Unspecified
| ^	Bitwise OR Bitwise XOR	L–R L–R	Unspecified Unspecified
&&	Logical AND	L–R	L–R

‖	Logical OR	L–R	L–R
?:	Conditional expr	R–L	Unspecified
=	Assignment	R–L	Unspecified
*=	Multiply assignment		
/=	Divided assignment		
%=	Modulus assignment		
+=	Add assignment		
−=	Subtract assignment		
<<=	Left shift assignment		
>>=	Right shift assignment		
&=	Bitwise AND assignment		
^=	Bitwise XOR assignment		
|=	Bitwise OR assignment		
,	Comma	L–R	L–R

converted automatically to the type of the variable on the left-hand side for any of the simple data types you have seen so far. For example:

```
int i;
char c;
float f;
f = 'A' + 2;
i = f;
c = i;
f = c;
i = f + i * c;
```

The first three lines declare variables i, c and f to be of types **int, char** and **float** respectively. The fourth line is an expression. Table 8.1 shows that the add operator has higher precedence than the assignment operator and so will be evaluated first. Add is a binary operator and its two operands are the character constant 'A' and the numeric integer constant 2. As 'A' is a **char** value it will automatically be translated to the **int** value 65 (assuming the use of the ASCII code). The constant 2 is already an **int** value so no further translations are necessary and the two values 65 and 2 can be added, giving the **int** result 67. Next the assignment operator is evaluated. The value of the right-hand operand (67) is translated to the type of the left-hand operand (variable f). So f is assigned the value 67.000000. Line 5 assigns the **float** value in variable f to the integer variable i. This involves the truncation of the value of f to make it the same type as i. The variable i is therefore assigned the integer value 67.

Line 6 assigns the **int** value in variable i to the **char** variable c. This means cutting the value of i to make it into an 8-bit **char** value. The **int** value 67 becomes the **char** value C (again assuming the use of the ASCII code).

Line 7, in evaluating the expression that is the right-hand operand of the assignment operator, will automatically translate the **char** value C into an **int** value (67). This is then converted by the assignment operator into a **float** value (67.000 000) to be reassigned to variable f.

The final line in the example is an expression containing three operators. The highest precedence operator is the multiply with operands i and c. The **char** value of c is translated to **int** and then the two **int** values can be multiplied to give (67*67) 4489. This leaves two operators to be evaluated. The highest precedence operator now is the add operator. Its two operands are the **float** value of variable f and the integer result of the previous multiply operation 4489. First the **float** value is translated to **double** and then the **int** value is translated to **double** also. The addition is now performed giving the **double** result 4556.000 000. Finally, in assigning this value to variable i it is truncated to the integer 4556.

Functions and arguments | 9

The use of functions allows you to split a large program into smaller pieces. This has many advantages as each function can be individually designed, written and tested, improving program maintainability. It allows libraries of previously written, tried and trusted functions to be accumulated and used over and over wherever appropriate. It also allows one programmer to call another programmer's functions knowing only their input parameter and output value specifications.

9.1 COMMUNICATING VALUES

In general, a C program is just a set of function definitions. Communication of values between functions is by one of three different methods. Values can be passed into a function by specifying parameters when a function is called. You saw this method in use when **printf** was called in the "Hello, world" program.

Functions are not just limited to taking one parameter, either. In fact, **printf** itself is much more sophisticated than you have seen so far, for as well as printing strings, **printf** can also be used for printing numbers. In its simplest form, integer values can be printed as follows:

printf("%d",i);

where **i** can be any expression that evaluates to an integer result. Notice in this example that **printf** has two parameters passed to it. These are separated by commas. Do not worry about the reason for the "**%d**" parameter. It and the rest of **printf**'s many facilities will be more fully explored in Section 12.3. For now it is sufficient to be able to print strings of characters and integer values.

In the second communication method a value can be passed back from a function as a result of its operation. Remember that the full general form of a function definition appears as follows:

type name(parameter list)

parameter declarations;

{

      function body;

}

When a function is required to return a value, then **type** in the above definition is the type of value that will be returned. For example, a function that
takes an integer value as a parameter and returns twice this value as its result:

```
int twice(n)
int n;
{
        return(n*2);
}
```

This is the definition of a function called **twice**. It takes as input a single
parameter, here given the local name **n**. The value of the parameter **n** is
declared to be of type **int**. The function is also declared to return a value of
type **int**. The value itself is produced by the **return** statement in the
function body. The execution of the **return** statement causes the termination of a function and returns the value of the expression in the brackets as
the value of the function.

```
main()
{
        int i,j,twice();

        i=10;
        j=twice(i);
}
```

This **main** function declares two **int** variables **i** and **j**. It also declares that the
function **twice()** returns an **int** value. The variable **i** is then assigned the
value 10. This value of **i** is next passed as a parameter to the function **twice**.
Inside function **twice** the parameter value is doubled and returned to the
calling function (here **main**). Inside **main** the value returned by **twice** is
assigned to the variable **j**.

It is good practice to declare the type returned by a function both in the
function definition and in the places where the function is called. In general
these declarations of function return value type are required. The only
exception to this rule is for functions that return type **int**. In these cases if no

type is declared then the function return value will automatically default to type **int**. So in the case of the **twice** example it would be sufficient to write:

```
main()
{
        int i,j;

        i=10;
        j=twice(i);
}

twice(n)        /* defaults to int */
int n;
{
        return(n*2);
}
```

Notice that comments can be inserted into C programs just by placing the comment text between the symbols /* and */. It is acceptable to place a comment anywhere that a white space character (space or '\t' or '\n') may legally appear, and it is good programming practice to make liberal use of them.

Declaring a variable inside a function makes the variable local to the function and generally inaccessible to other parts of the program. For example, in the previous program variables **i** and **j** are local **int** variables to the function **main** and variable **n** is a local **int** variable to function **twice**. Local variables are allocated space dynamically at program run time. They are created when a function is entered and destroyed when it exits or returns. In the function **main** there is no access to the variable **n** in **twice** and similarly function **twice** cannot directly access **i** or **j** in **main**. Any attempt to access the local variables of one function directly from within another function, as in:

```
twice()
{
        return(i*2);
}
```

where **twice** tries directly to access the variable **i** in **main**, will result in an error message being issued to say that a local variable i has not been declared within **twice** and so cannot be used. Sometimes it can be useful to be able to access variables from within two or more functions that are common to them all and this idea provides the third communication mechanism between functions. These special variables are declared to be global to all the functions in a particular source code file by declaring them outside of any of the functions:

```
int i;        /* global variable i */

main()
{
        int j;
        i=10;
        j=twice();
}


twice()       /* no parameter passed */
{
        return(i*2);
}
```

Here the **int** variable **i** is declared outside of the functions **main** and **twice** and this makes the variable global and accessible to both. Function **main** sets **i** to the value 10 and then calls **twice**. Function **twice** needs no parameters passed to it as the value for it to work on is now communicated in a different way. The function picks up its working value from the global variable **i** and returns twice this value in the usual way. Notice that with global variables several functions may use them and so they must not be created and destroyed as each function begins and ends. Rather than being dynamically created at run time, global variables need to be static so that their values can be maintained between functions.

9.2 STORAGE CLASSES

In C there are four standard storage classes that specify how variables are to be treated and when they will be accessible. The first is called **automatic** and variables of this class are local variables declared within functions. They are called automatic because they are automatically created and destroyed as functions execute and terminate. The second basic storage class that a variable can be assigned to in a C program is called **register**. A variable is declared to belong to the register storage class just by adding the word **register** in front of the normal declaration of a local variable:

fcn1()

{

     register int i;

     ____

}

Here the variable **i** is declared to be a **register int**. During program execution the variable **i** will behave just as though it had been declared as an ordinary automatic local **int**. The difference is that the **register** declaration tells the compiler that you think the variable **i** will be particularly heavily used within the function where it has been declared. If possible the compiler should take the opportunity to store the value of register variables in internal processor registers (hence the name) rather than out in memory, because in general the values in processor registers can be accessed much faster than equivalent values in memory. Obviously, the number of registers available for this purpose inside any particular processor is strictly limited and so only the most important variable values should use the **register** declaration. Any variables that are declared to be of class **register** for which a processor register is not available are treated just as ordinary local **automatic** variables.

The third storage class is called **extern**. This is because variables of this class are declared external to any function. External variables retain their values throughout the execution of a program. Global variables (i.e. those that are declared outside of any function) are set to storage class **extern** by default. Sometimes it can be useful to have a variable that is local to a particular function but which does not lose its value between calls of the function. That is, it should be a variable local to one function but with the other attributes of an **extern** variable. In cases like this it is possible to declare the variable to be **static** within the function instead of allowing the compiler to have it created and destroyed each time the function is called.

Storage class **static** is the fourth and final variable class:

```
total(n)
int n;
{
        static int t;

        return(t+=n);
}
```

Here the variable **t** is declared to be a **static int** so that it will not lose its value between calls of the function **total**.

What the function **total** does is to take the value of the parameter passed into it, and add that value to the existing value of variable **t**. The new value of **t** is returned by total as its result.

Only two questions remain concerning function **total**. What is the value of **t** before **total** is first called, and how could this value be set to something else if required?

9.3 VARIABLE INITIALIZATION

When a variable is defined it occupies one or more locations of memory. Before a value is assigned to a variable its value is whatever is contained in the memory locations it occupies. In the case of **automatic** variables this value can be anything — it is just whatever was in the memory locations from any previous usage of the space. With **extern** and **static** variables, however, the memory locations are fixed throughout the execution of the program and the compiler automatically arranges for these locations to hold the value 0 as a default starting value. This means that as the program stands the variable **t** in the function **total** is always guaranteed to start off with a 0 value.

If for any reason it was desirable to start off a variable of any type with a value other than 0 then this can be done by initialization:

```
product(n)
int n;
{
        static int p=1;

        return(p*=n);
}
```

The function **product** above performs a similar job to the function **total** in the previous example except that instead of adding the parameter value into an accumulating total it is multiplied into an accumulating product. In this case if the **static** variable holding the accumulating result started off with the value 0 then this is the only value that the function would ever return. To overcome the problem the **static** variable (**p** in this case) needs to be initialized to 1 instead of 0. This is done on the line in which the variable is declared just by adding an equals sign and the initial value after the variable name.

9.4 STANDARD C FUNCTIONS

So far the only standard C library function you have seen is **printf** and even this was only lightly skipped over. There are many more library functions than this and if you are to write useful programs the first ones to look at are those that provide simple input from the keyboard (or standard input device) and output to the screen (or standard output device).

All input and output under UNIX including that from the keyboard and to the screen are treated as though you were accessing a file. Normally a connection has to be made between your program and any file it needs to access. (This will be covered in Chapter 12.) But in the case of the standard input and output devices the files are opened by the shell before it runs your program. The shell will open the keyboard and the screen as the default I/O devices unless the standard input or output has been redirected, on the command line to the shell with the input (<) or output (>) redirection operators or by the use of a pipe (|). As the standard I/O devices are opened for use automatically, these are the easiest devices to use.

9.4.1 Getchar and putchar

The simplest way to read characters from the standard input device is to use **getchar**:

int c;

c=getchar( );

Here **getchar** acts like a function which takes a character from the standard input and returns its value which is then assigned to the **int** variable **c**.

When you have a character to print, the simplest way to print it to the standard output is to use **putchar**:

int c;

c=getchar( );

putchar(c);

Here the character to output is passed to **putchar** as a parameter in the brackets.

9.5. INCLUDING FILES

In order to be able to use **getchar** and **putchar** in your programs along with quite a few other facilities it is necessary to include the contents of a standard C header file called **stdio.h**. It would be very tedious if the contents of this file had to be typed or copied into each of your programs before you could use some useful facilities. Fortunately this is not the case as the contents of the file can be added to your program by the C compiler itself using a command to the compiler to do so. All you need to do is to add the line:

#include <stdio.h>

at the start of your program and the contents of the file will automatically be included. You do not even need to know which directory in the file system contains the file (usually **/usr/include**) as enclosing the file name in angle brackets instructs the compiler to search the system default directory. You can also use the **#include** command to have the contents of your own files added to your programs. If you enclose the file name in double quotes instead of angle brackets then the file can be in any specified directory:

#include "/usr/pc/src/myfile"

9.6 TEXT SUBSTITUTION

The **#include** command is not the only **#** command available in C. Another very useful one allows you to give a name to a block of text. Whenever the specified name appears in the body of your program then the name is substituted by the compiler for the specified block of text. The new command is called **#define** and its simplest and most common usage is to allow you to give a symbolic name to a numeric constant value. The practice makes your programs easier to read, if the names and values are well chosen, and is strongly recommended:

#define YES 1

#define NO 0

#define RANDOM_SEED 92177

In the above example wherever any of the names YES, NO or RANDOM_SEED appear in your program it will be removed and one of the values 1, 0 or 92177 respectively will be substituted in its place. The **#define** command is not just limited to defining simple numeric values:

#define HARD_SUM (a+b)*(c+d)/(2*a)

would substitute the whole of the expression $(a+b)^*(c+d)/(2^*a)$ for each occurrence of the name HARD_SUM.

Two things to notice are that all the names used have been in upper case. This is not a mandatory rule but it is an almost universal convention and to avoid confusion with variable names, etc. you should try to follow the convention. And, second, is that like **#include**s, the **#define** lines do not end with a semicolon unless you want to have a semicolon substituted for the name along with the rest of the text.

A very simple program example now, using some of this new information, will take a single character from the keyboard and assuming that it is a lower-case letter will translate it into the equivalent upper-case letter:

```
#include <stdio.h>

#define LITTLEA 'a'
#define BIGA 'A'
#define NEWLINE '\n'

main( )
{
        int c,d;

        c = getchar( );
        d = c - LITTLEA + BIGA;
        putchar(d);
        putchar(NEWLINE);
}
```

There are two points to note about this program example. The first point concerns the expression statement:

d = c − LITTLEA + BIGA;

When the text substitution has been performed this expression becomes:

d = c − 'a' + 'A';

What does it mean to add the letter 'A' in an expression? If you remember in Chapter 8, I said that any character constant (i.e. a character enclosed in single quotes) was actually stored as a number whose value is the numeric representation of the specified character in the machine's standard character set (either ASCII or EBCDIC). So on a machine using the ASCII character set for example, adding the character constant 'A' is the same as adding the decimal value 65 (as 65 is the ASCII code for the upper-case letter A). But how does this help to convert lower case to upper case? Suppose that the letter you want to convert is the lower-case letter 'a'. The code for 'a' is assigned to the variable **c** and from this is subtracted the character constant 'a'. Obviously it does not matter what character code is being used, evaluating the expression:

'a' − 'a'

gives 0 as the result. If the character constant 'A' is now added then the final result assigned to variable **d** will be 'A' as required. This seems rather a trivial example so let us examine another. Convert the letter 'c'. This value is assigned to **c** and the character constant 'a' is subtracted. If the characters in the character code are numbered sequentially so that 'a' is followed by 'b' which is followed by 'c', etc. then the expression:

'c' − 'a'

gives the value 2. Again assuming that 'A' is followed by 'B' which is followed by 'C', etc. then adding 2 to the character constant 'A' should give the value of the character 'C', i.e. the required result. Those of you who know the ASCII code will know that it is laid out in the way that I have assumed. Unfortunately the EBCDIC code is not so obliging and there are some gaps in the code. When you examine the situation closer, however, you discover that as long as each of the lower-case letters is as far away in the code from its corresponding upper-case letter as 'a' is from 'A' then the method will still work unchanged. And this test is passed by the EBCDIC code so that this method may be used for that code as well as ASCII

The second point to notice is that the result of the **getchar** function, which returns a **char** value from the standard input, is being assigned to an **int** variable **c**. You remember I said that all input and output under UNIX are via files. When all the data has been read from a file then you will get an end of file (EOF) condition if you try to read the file again. The EOF condition from the keyboard occurs when you press ctrl–d. Any subsequent use of **getchar** will return an EOF value (EOF is predefined in the file **stdio.h** which has been **#include**d into the program). If the value of EOF was just one of the 256 possible **char** values then there would be no way to distinguish it from the equivalent **char** value. Therefore, EOF is arranged to return a value that is outside the **char** range but inside the **int** range and so the value that is returned from **getchar** should be assigned to an **int** variable so that EOF may be detected.

Program flow control | 10

The control of program flow in C as with many other languages is generally sequential. This means that in general the lines of code in a C program execute one after another in the order that they are encountered. This rule continues to be the case unless a specific flow control construct is encountered which then may or may not alter the sequential flow. Generally the normal flow is altered based on the result of some test condition which is used to determine by its value what action should be taken next.

Apart from the normal sequential flow control sequence there are two other types of flow control sequences. One is called selection where one or more possible execution paths are available and a test condition selects which path is executed. The other is called iteration where a single execution path is available but this path will be executed repeatedly until some test condition fails to be met when the iteration terminates.

If an executable statement is represented diagrammatically as the simple block in Fig. 10.1 then a sequence of statements would appear as in Fig. 10.2 where the arrows represent the direction of execution flow.

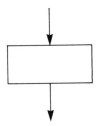

Fig. 10.1 A representation of a single executable statement.

10.1 IF STATEMENTS

The simplest selection construct is the **if** statement. The syntax of the **if** statement is:

if (condition)

    statement

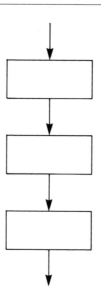

Fig. 10.2 Three statements in SEQUENCE

The condition contained within the brackets is just a numeric expression. If the condition expression evaluates to a non-zero (TRUE) value then the following single statement is executed. If the condition value is zero (FALSE) then the controlled statement is skipped. Diagrammatically this can be seen as in Fig. 10.3. Notice that the syntax only allows for a single statement to be controlled by the **if** construct. If more than one statement needs to be executed then they can be enclosed within open and closed curly brackets:

```
{
    statement;
    statement;
    statement;
}
```

This arrangement is called a compound statement and syntactically it counts just as a single statement. Sometimes you may wish to perform one action if the condition expression is TRUE and another action if it is FALSE. This situation can still be catered for using the **if** statement but with an optional **else** clause:

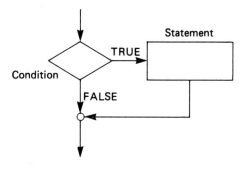

Fig. 10.3 Layout of an 'if' statement

if (condition)

    statement1

else

    statement2

Again in diagrammatic form this appears as in Fig. 10.4. It is possible to nest these **if** statements one within another by allowing the controlled statement of one **if** construct itself to be another **if**:

if (condition1)

    if (condition2)

        statement

This says that if condition1 is TRUE then the controlled statement should be executed. The controlled statement here is another **if** which says if condition2 is TRUE then execute its controlled statement. So that in effect the inner statement is not executed unless both condition1 and condition2 are TRUE at the same time (see Fig. 10.5). Unfortunately, because the **else** clause of an **if** statement is optional it causes an ambiguity to use an **else** clause after a pair of nested **if** statements. For example does the program line:

if (a) if (b) c; else d;

where a, b, c and d are any standard C expressions, mean:

```
if (a)
    if (b)
        c;
    else
        d;
```

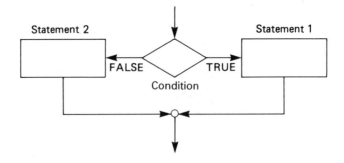

Fig. 10.4 The 'if' statement with optional 'else' clause

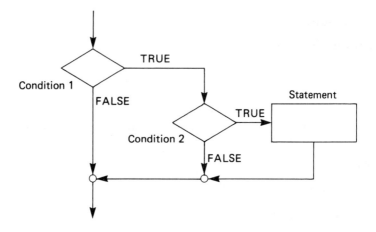

Fig. 10.5 Nested 'if' statements

or does it mean:

```
if (a)
     if (b)
          c;
else
     d;
```

In other words, does the **else** match up with the first **if** or the second? In order to resolve this ambiguity C provides a simple rule which clears things up. The **else** belongs to the closest unmatched **if**. In the example this is the second **if** statement (i.e. the **if** (b) statement) which corresponds to the first of the two possibilities above. Using the **if–else** statement it is now possible to rewrite the lower-case to upper-case translator program from Chapter 9 so

that it only performs any sort of translation action on characters in the range
'a' to 'z':

```
#include <stdio.h>

main()
{
        int c;

        c = getchar();

        if (c >= 'a' && c <= 'z')
                putchar(c - 'a' + 'A');
        else
                putchar(c);

        putchar('\n');
}
```

The first statement uses **getchar** to get a character into **c**. This character is
then checked by the **if** condition to see if it is in the range 'a' to 'z'. If it is,
then the value of **c** is translated to upper case using the formula you have
seen before and then output using **putchar**. If the value of **c** is not a lower-
case letter then the **else** clause is used and the value of **c** is printed
unchanged. Finally, whichever path is taken through the **if–else** construct a
newline character ('\n') is printed at the end.

10.2 WHILE LOOPS

The first and most simple of the iteration statements is the **while** loop, the
general syntax for which is:

while (condition)

    statement

What happens here is that the condition expression is evaluated and if the
result is TRUE then the controlled statement is executed. So far this sounds
like the **if** statement. The difference, however, is that after the controlled
statement is executed the program flow loops back to the **while** and re-
evaluates the condition. If the condition is still TRUE then the controlled
statement is executed again. Program execution continues to iterate around
this loop until eventually the condition expression returns the value FALSE at
which time the controlled statement is skipped and execution continues with
the next statement (see Fig. 10.6). Just as with the **if** construct, the **while**
construct can only control a single statement, unless a compound block is
used (statements enclosed in curly brackets):

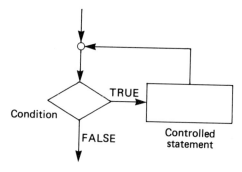

Fig. 10.6 ITERATION with the test at the top of the loop

while (condition)

{

   statement

   statement

   ____

}

Using the **while** construct it is now possible to perform a set of actions repeatedly. Again using the lower-case to upper-case translation example, it is possible using **while** to have the translation process applied repeatedly to the entire contents of a file from the start of the file up to the receipt of the EOF condition:

```
#include <stdio.h>

main( )
{
        int c;

        while ((c = getchar()) != EOF)
               if (c >= 'a' && c <= 'z')
                       putchar(c - 'a' + 'A');
               else
                       putchar(c);
}
```

Notice that the whole **if–else** construct only counts as a single statement as far as the **while** construct is concerned so that curly brackets are not required around the **if–else** statement. If you are ever in any doubt about whether curly brackets are needed or not it is always acceptable to use them even where they are not strictly necessary.

Another point about this program that is worth a mention is the **while** condition expression:

((c = getchar( )) != EOF)

At the end of the evaluation, this expression needs to yield either a TRUE or FALSE value so that the decision can be made whether to execute the controlled statement or not. However, evaluation begins with the contents of the inner brackets:

(c = getchar( ))

This is an assignment operator which will call **getchar** to get a character from the standard input and assign the result to the variable **c**. You remember that the value returned by an assignment operator is the value that is assigned to the variable on the left of the operator. So the value assigned to **c** is then compared to the value of EOF. If the two values are not the same, so that EOF has not been reached, the condition expression returns the value TRUE and the character in variable **c** is used by the controlled statement. Eventually the two values will be the same when the EOF is reached and then the condition expression will be FALSE and the **while** loop terminates.

As the program is written, input will normally come from the keyboard and output will be sent to the screen. Under UNIX using I/O redirection, the same program can be made to take its standard input from a file and also return its output to a file if required. If the program is called **translate** then:

$ translate < translate.c

will read the source code for the command redirected in from the file **translate.c** and send the translated version to the screen.

10.3 FOR LOOPS

Another iteration construct in C that is very similar to the **while** loop is called **for**. In quite a lot of programming situations where iteration is involved there is a need to perform some sort of initialization on a variable before the loop begins and a need to perform some kind of incremental action at the end of the body of the loop before the loop termination condition is evaluated again. The **for** loop provides both of these extra facilities in addition to the facilities provided by the simple **while** loop. The general format of the **for** loop construct is:

for (init; condition; inc)

   statement

As usual with C flow control constructs, the **for** construct can only control a single statement or a compound statement in curly brackets. Notice that in the case of **for** the brackets contain three separate expressions separated by semicolons. The first of these is the initialization expression which is evaluated before the main loop begins. The second is a termination condition which has exactly the same form as the equivalent condition in a **while** loop in that if the condition expression evaluates to TRUE then the controlled statement will be executed and if the condition is FALSE then the **for** loop terminates. The third expression is the incremental step and this expression is evaluated each time the condition expression is TRUE, just after execution of the controlled statement. From this description it should be clear that in general the **for** loop:

for (a; b; c)

> **statement**

is exactly equivalent to the **while** loop:

a;

while (b)

{

> **statement**
>
> **c;**

}

Any or all of the three expressions in the **for** loop can be omitted. If the initialization or incremental expressions are omitted then these actions are just not performed. If the conditional expression is omitted then it is taken to have been an expression that evaluated to TRUE. This means that the loop will never terminate without making some special arrangements. The general format for the infinite loop in C then is:

for (;;)

> **statement**

Notice that even when the expressions are absent it is still necessary to include the semicolons. Another possibility which makes the meaning clearer is to use the **#define** facility with the following definition:

#define ever (;;)

which then allows infinite loops to be coded as:

for ever

> **statement**

An example program using a **for** loop to print out the letters of the alphabet in ascending order is:

```
#include <stdio.h>

main()
{
        char c;

        for (c = 'a'; c <= 'z'; c++)
                putchar(c);
}
```

Remember that this **for** loop is equivalent to:

c = 'a';

while (c < = 'z')

{

   putchar(c);

   c++;

}

The program initializes variable **c** to the value 'a', the first letter of the alphabet, and then iterates round the loop printing and incrementing **c** until the whole alphabet has been printed. This particular program relies on the letters of the alphabet following each other in the machine's underlying character code in ascending order. This is true for the ASCII code but **not** for EBCDIC. On an EBCDIC machine therefore the program would need some modification to make it work correctly.

10.4 DO–WHILE LOOPS

Both the **while** and **for** loops that you have just seen have one thing in common – they both perform evaluation of the conditional expression before executing the controlled statement. This is perfect for most applications but sometimes it is more convenient if the controlled statement is executed first and then followed by conditional expression evaluation to determine whether to iterate back to the controlled statement or not. This order of evaluation is provided in C by the **do–while** construct. The general format of the statement is:

do

    statement

while (condition);

Diagrammatically this appears as in Fig. 10.7. Notice that the difference between **while** and **do–while** is that in the **while** case the controlled statement need not be executed at all if the conditional expression returns the value FALSE on first evaluation. Whereas in the **do–while** case the controlled statement will always be executed at least once because the conditional expression is not evaluated until after this first execution.

    As an example of the use of **do–while** consider the following listing:

```
#include <stdio.h>

main()
{
        int c;

        do
        {
                c = getchar();
                putchar(c);
        }
        while (c != '\n');
}
```

Here, characters are being copied from the standard input device to the standard output device up to and including the first newline character (\n). As you can see, the single statement specified in the general format of the

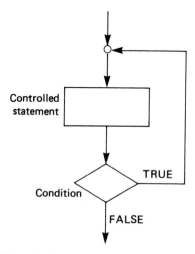

Fig. 10.7 ITERATION with the test at the bottom of the loop

do—while construct may be replaced by a compound statement block in curly brackets.

Notice that because the controlled statements are executed before the condition is evaluated, when a newline is returned by **getchar** it will be output by **putchar** before the condition terminates the loop. To achieve the same effect with **while** would require a much more clumsy program:

```
#include <stdio.h>

main()
{
        int c;

        c = getchar();
        putchar(c);
        while (c != '\n')
        {
                c = getchar();
                putchar(c);
        }
}
```

Notice that the body of the **while** loop has to be repeated outside the loop to ensure that its action is always performed before evaluation of the termination condition.

10.4.1 continue

This is a flow control statement that is only of any use inside one of the three iterative loops (**while, for** and **do—while**). When the statement is encountered it causes early termination of the current iteration of the enclosing loop, continuing execution with the next iteration. In the case of **while** and **do—while** loops the next iteration begins with re-evaluation of the termination condition. In the case of the **for** loop it means execution of the incremental step before re-evaluation of the termination condition:

for (i = 6; i >= (−6); i−−)

{

    if (i == 0)   /* skip 0 value */

        continue;

    /* **process non zero values of i** */

}

In the above example only non-zero values of the variable **i** are used for processing within the loop. The zero case is weeded out by the **continue** statement.

10.5 SWITCH-CASE

There are many occasions when the value of a variable needs to be tested and one of several actions taken depending upon the result. For example, when a user enters a command letter into **ed** the editor has to test the value and branch to one of several functions to deal with the user's requirements:

```
if (cmd == 'a')
        /* process append */
else if (cmd == 'c')
        /* process change */
else if (cmd == 'd')
        /* process delete */
else if (cmd == 'e')
        /* process edit file */

etc ...
```

The **switch** construct is a way to achieve the same result without all the tedious nested **if–else** statements. As you can see, a complete expression has to be evaluated in an **if** test for every possible value of the variable **cmd** and this is quite an overhead. It would be much better just to examine the contents of **cmd** and then branch directly to a routine to deal with the required command. This is exactly what **switch** does:

```
switch (cmd)
{
case 'a':
        /* process append */
case 'c':
        /* process change */
case 'd':
        /* process delete */
case 'e'
        /* process edit file */
etc ...

}
```

The **switch** statement evaluates the integer expression in the brackets to give an integer result. Each **case** within the curly brackets is then labelled with an integer or character constant or constant expression followed by a colon. Execution passes directly from the **switch** statement to the **case** whose label value matches the evaluated test expression. (This appears diagrammatically in Fig. 10.8.)

Notice that the code for all the **cases** forms a single compound statement enclosed within curly brackets. Also notice that the **switch** mechanism only provides one of several entry points into this block of code and no method for early termination of the block. This is why Fig. 10.8 shows the blocks of code for the **cases** running into each other. As things stand, once an entry point has been selected all the code after that point will be executed. This means that if 'd' is selected to delete a block of text then after the code to delete the block

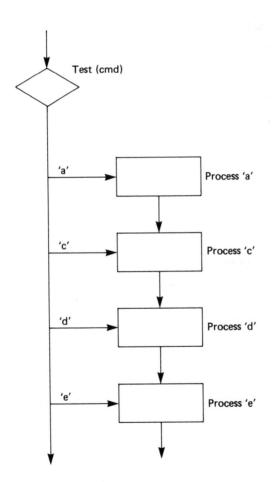

Fig. 10.8 Operation of the 'switch/case' statement

has run, execution passes to the block of code to process 'e' and so on to the end of the **switch** construct. There are occasions when this can be useful but mostly you will want to terminate the **switch** early when each of the **cases** has done its job.

10.5.1 break

This early termination of **cases** can be achieved with the **break** statement which just causes the enclosing construct to terminate directly without any further execution of the enclosing construct's statements:

switch (cmd)

{

case 'a':

      /* process append */

      break;

case 'c':

      /* process change */

      break;

case 'd':

      /* process delete */

      break;

etc − − − − −

default:

      /* no match so error */

}

Using **break**, execution of the **switch** construct is modified as shown in Fig. 10.9 and this is generally much more useful.

Obviously, the possibility exists with the **switch** statement that the value of the test expression does not match any of the **case** labels. To cope with this possibility, C provides a special label called **default:** and this is the label that will be reached if no other match is found. Use of the **break** statement is not just confined to the **switch** construct. It can also be used to the same effect with the **while, for** and **do−while** constructs; that is, each of these constructs is immediately terminated when **break** is encountered.

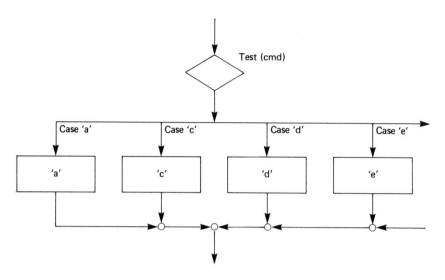

Fig. 10.9 using 'break' with 'switch' gives a SELECTION construct

10.6 goto STATEMENTS

So far, each of the constructs you have considered has only had one way into it and one way out. This leads to programs that are generally easier to read and to maintain. However, C does provide a statement that can so easily be misused and upset these desirable features — **goto**. In theory there are no situations where the use of a **goto** statement is necessary. And even in practice the number of real uses for **goto**s is very limited. What the **goto** statement does is unconditionally to transfer control of program execution to a specified line. For example:

goto identifier;

where identifier is the name of a label that appears somewhere within the currently executing function. Any statement in a C program can be labelled as the target of a **goto** statement just by prefixing it with an identifier followed by a colon:

identifier:

   statement

Label identifiers in C have the same syntax as variable names but they do not need to be declared other than by their appearance in the program followed by a colon.

   Notice from the above that labels are local to a particular function body so that a **goto** in one function cannot access a label in another function. The only really practical use for the **goto** statement is to escape out of the middle of a nest of loop constructs, say under error conditions:

```
while (————————————)
{
        while (————————————)
        {
                if(error())
                        goto end;

                ————————————

                ————————————
        }
}
return (OK);
end: /* deal with error here */
        return (BAD);
```

Notice that **break** cannot easily be used in this case because it would only terminate the innermost loop.

10.6.1 Program examples

Some surprisingly sophisticated programs can be produced with only the knowledge of C that you have so far. I shall end this chapter with a few simple examples.

10.6.2 Word counting

You remember back in Chapter 3 the use of a standard UNIX command called **wc**, whose function is to count the number of lines, words and characters in its input stream until EOF is encountered. You have ample knowledge now to write a slightly simplified version of this command. All you have to do is to decide what exactly it is that constitutes a line, a word and a character and then arrange to have these items counted in three separate variables. Taking a character to be anything returned by **getchar** up to but not including EOF, a line to be any consecutive block of characters up to a '\n' character and a word to be any consecutive block of characters that does not contain any of the characters' space, '\t' or '\n', gives the following possible program:

```
#include <stdio.h>

#define TRUE 1
#define FALSE 0

main()
{
        int cc,wc,lc;
        int inword,c;

        cc = wc = lc = 0;
        inword = FALSE;

        while ((c = getchar()) != EOF)
        {
                cc++;
                if (c == '\n')
                        lc++;

                if (c == '\t' || c == ' ' || c == '\n')
                        inword = FALSE;
                else
                        if (inword == FALSE)
                        {
                                wc++;
                                inword = TRUE;
                        }
        }
        printf("line count=");
        printf("%d",lc);
        printf("\nword count=");
        printf("%d",wc);
        printf("\ncharacter count=");
        printf("%d",cc);
        printf("\n");
}
```

Here three variables are declared to hold the three important values, number of lines (**lc**), number of words (**wc**) and number of characters (**cc**). Two more variables are also declared, the first (**inword**) is a flag to specify whether the current character is part of a word or not. The second (**c**) is just used to hold the character values as they are read in by **getchar**. Next the variables are initialized. Then the main loop of the program is entered. The main loop is a **while** construct which reads characters with **getchar**, assigns them to **c** and then tests them for EOF. While the value of **c** is not equal to EOF the body of the loop is executed. The actions in the loop are to increment the character count (**cc**) and if the current character is a newline (\n) to increment the line count (**lc**). Finally an **if-else** construct is used to sort out a count of words. What this does is to count the number of times a sequence of white space characters ('', '\t' or '\n') ends and a word begins. To do this the variable **inword** is set to FALSE every time a white space character is encountered. Then whenever **inword** is FALSE and the current character is not white space, a new word must have started, so **inword** is set to TRUE and the word count (**wc**) is incremented. Finally, on EOF the values of the three count variables are printed with **printf** statements.

10.6.3 Listing funny files

There are many occasions when you will want to list the contents of a file but you do not know if it contains pure text or a mixture of text and odd control codes which may lock up your video terminal if listed. What you need is a facility for listing programs like **cat** but which transforms the control codes into something harmless to your video terminal (like a dot '.' for example):

```
#include <stdio.h>
main()
{
        int c;

        while ((c = getchar()) != EOF)
                if (c < ' ' || c > '}')
                        putchar('.');
                else
                        putchar(c);
}
```

This program is arranged to operate on files stored using the ASCII code. All ASCII codes between the space and the closed curly bracket are printable and can be sent to the terminal unchanged. Characters with codes outside this range may cause problems on some terminals and are thus translated into a dot (.). This is repeated until EOF is encountered.

Just suppose that you wanted to write a function which would swap the values of two variables. You might try something like the following:

```
swap1(a,b)
int a,b;
{
        int t;

        t = a;
        a = b;
        b = t;
}
```

As you can see, the function **swap1** takes two parameters **a** and **b** of type **int**. Using a third temporary **int** variable, **t**, the values of **a** and **b** are swapped over.

What would be the result, then, of calling the function **swap1** from the following **main** function?

```
main()
{
        int x,y;

        x = 12;
        y = 24;

        swap(x,y);
        printf("%d\n",x);
        printf("%d\n",y);
}
```

What will the values of **x** and **y** be when they are output by the **printf** statements? (Try it!)

If you tried it you will have discovered that **x** still has the value 12 and **y** the value 24, which are the values they were initialized with. Does this mean that **swap1** does not work?

In fact **swap1** works perfectly in that the values of **x** and **y** are copied into the local parameter variables **a** and **b** respectively. The values of **a** and **b** are then swapped over via the temporary variable **t** and **swap1** then terminates as expected. And yet **x** and **y** in the calling function remain unchanged.

This is because parameters in C are only passed by value and not by reference. What this means is that only the values of parameter expressions are passed into functions and that a function's internal parameter variables are purely local to the function so that changing the values of the internal parameter variables does not affect values in the calling function.

11.1 POINTERS

How then can a swap function be written so that actions within the called function can affect the values of variables in the calling function? The answer is to use **pointers**. A pointer in C is just an address of some location in memory. These address values can be stored in variables which have been declared to be pointer variables:

int i,*pi;

This line declares two variables, one called **i** which is an ordinary **int** and the other called **pi** which, because of the asterisk (*) in front of it, is declared to be a **pointer** to an **int**. Notice that it is not sufficient just to declare **pi** to be a **pointer**. In some circumstances (that you will see later) the compiler actually needs to know what type of object the **pointer** is supposed to be pointing at. A **pointer** variable is said to be 'pointing at' an object when the variable contains the address of that object.

The address of an object can be found by using the unary ampersand (**&**) operator. (I know that ampersand (**&**) is also used as the bitwise OR operator. But bitwise OR is a binary operator so you can always tell one from the other by the context in which it appears.)

Here is an expression whose value is the address in memory of the variable **i**:

&i

This address value can be assigned to a **pointer** variable of the correct type as follows:

pi = &i;

Here the previously declared integer pointer (**pi**) is assigned the address of **i**. And so after this line has executed, **pi** points at **i**.

The use of pointers would not be justified unless there was some way to use them to access the value of the object that they point at. And indeed there is — another unary operator (this time the asterisk (*) is used) is available to do just that:

*pi

This is an expression that returns the value of the object that the variable **pi** is pointing at. Since at this time **pi** is pointing at the variable **i**, the above expression returns the value of **i**.

Given the following sequence:

int i,j,*pi;

i = 10;

pi = &i;

j = *pi;

the variables **i** and **j** both end up with the same value (i.e. 10). I appreciate that this sequence is equivalent to the line:

j = i = 10;

which is the way that the assignment would normally be done, but in some cases pointers really come into their own — the **swap** function for example.

Using pointers you have a method of passing a value into a function that can be used to access an object outside the function via its address in memory.

Rewriting the **swap** function so that the two parameters are pointers to two **int** variables, and then exchanging the values of these two variables using the pointers gives:

```
swap2(pa,pb)
int *pa,*pb;
{
        int t;

        t = *pa;
        *pa = *pb;
        *pb = t;
}
```

Now you have a function which, because it is dealing with the addresses of two variables in the calling function, can by use of the addresses indirectly modify the variable values. An example of a **main** function to call the new **swap2** could be:

```
main()
{
        int x,y;

        x = 12;
        y = 24;

        swap2(&x,&y);
        printf("%d\n",x);
        printf("%d\n",y);
}
```

address

Notice that the parameters passed into **swap2** are the addresses of the variables **x** and **y** this time and not their values as before. This time the **printf** statements at the end of **main** will show **x** to have a value of 24 and **y** a value of 12 as expected.

Having executed a statement like:

pi = &i;

then the expression:

*pi

can be used anywhere that the variable **i** itself could have been used. For example:

printf("%d",i);

is exactly equivalent to:

printf("%d",*pi);

11.2 ARRAYS

So far you have seen only simple variables, that is, a variable that can hold only a single value of a particular type such as an integer, a pointer or a character. Very often, however, you will be concerned with collections of data of various types. One of the simplest collections of data is an **array**. An array is a specified number of data elements all of the same type. For example:

int digit[10];

is a declaration of an array variable called **digit**. As you can see, **digit** has been declared to consist of 10 separate elements each of type **int**. This means that there are 10 **int** values all stored in the array data structure called **digit**. Obviously you will need a method of accessing the values stored in individual elements of the array. This is done by specifying an element subscript in square brackets after the array name:

digit[7] = 6;

printf("%d",digit[4]);

The declaration of **digit** above specified its size as 10 elements. In C the elements of an array always number from zero so that acceptable element subscripts for the **digit** array are from 0 to 9, giving the required 10 elements in all.

A simple example program using the **digit** array will read the standard input one character at a time until EOF is encountered and each time a character in the file in the range '0' to '9' is read the appropriate element of the **digit** array will be incremented. This will keep a count of the number of occurrences of each numeric digit in the input stream which can be printed out at the end:

```
#include <stdio.h>

main()
{
        int digit[10],c;

        while ((c = getchar()) != EOF)
                if (c >= '0' && c <= '9')
                        digit[c - '0']++;

        for (c = 0; c <= 9; c++)
                printf("%d\n",digit[c]);
}
```

EOF = CTRL+D
'\n' = equal to hitting return key

The only line in the program that might need some explanation is:

digit[c − '0']++;

Bear in mind that when the program encounters the digit '0' it needs to increment **digit [0]** by 1, when it encounters the digit '1' it needs to increment **digit [1]** and so on. This is exactly what the line above does. Remember that (c−'0') will translate the ASCII or EBCDIC codes for the digit characters '0' to '9' into integer values 0 to 9 which can then be used as subscripts into the **digit** array. So **digit[c−'0']** selects the correct array element and then the post-increment (++) operator on the end increments it by 1 as required.

11.3 ARRAY INITIALIZATION

You have already seen how ordinary variables of all storage classes can be initialized to fixed starting values. With arrays the situation is slightly different in that only static and external arrays may be initialized.

This can be done by following the declaration with an equal sign and a list of element values separated by commas and all enclosed within a pair of curly brackets:

static int factors[6] = {8,3,1,7,7,2};

Here, **factors[0]** will be set to 8, **factors[1]** will be set to 3 and so on.

When initialization is used it is acceptable to omit the size of the array in the declaration. In such cases the compiler will automatically work out the size of the array from the number of elements that are given initial values:

static int factors[ ] = {8,3,1,7,7,2};

Thus this is an equivalent declaration to the previous example.

11.4 STRINGS

By far the most common use for arrays in C is to hold strings of characters. Strings are generally stored one character per array element in consecutive elements of a **char** array. This means that the first character of the string is stored in array element 0, the second character in element 1 and so on. To act as a string terminator, it is usual to place a zero-valued element ('\0') at the end of the string. As you will see, in some cases C automatically terminates a string in this way. For example, whenever you specify a string literal (i.e. a string enclosed in double quotes) in a program it is automatically stored in consecutive memory locations in the program's static storage area and terminated by a zero byte. This means that each literal string occupies one more byte in memory than its actual length, to account for the terminator. This is exactly the way that the same string would be stored if the characters of the string were assigned to the elements of a **char** array and zero terminated. So in effect string literals are internally stored as **char** arrays. As an example of the use of a string literal consider the following line:

printf("This is a string literal\n");

where the string literal is the parameter to the **printf** library function. What sort of value is actually passed to **printf** when the parameter is evaluated?

Bear in mind that the **printf** function needs to be able to access the characters of the string from the addresses where they are stored in memory. And already I am sure you will not be surprised to discover that a pointer is involved. The actual value that is returned by C for a literal string is a pointer to its first byte in memory. The **printf** function in this case can use the pointer to access the characters of the string and print them out until the zero-valued element is encountered.

11.5 POINTER ARITHMETIC

So, if you pass an address to **printf** this will be assigned to a local parameter variable inside the function. Obviously, this parameter variable will be a pointer to char (say — char *param1;) and using the line:

putchar(*param1);

inside **printf** would allow the first character of the message to be printed. This is not in fact the way that **printf** works — it is much more complex — but I am only interested in the principle.

Okay, accessing the first character of the message was easy but what about the second and subsequent characters; how are they to be accessed?

Remember that the characters of the message are each stored in consecutive memory locations and that you have a pointer to the first location. All you need to do then is to advance the pointer on by one location to point to the next character and then print this character in the same way as the first. To do this requires the use of pointer arithmetic which allows pointers to be incremented and decremented in just the way required. So the line:

param1++;

will advance the pointer **param1** so that it points one character further on, that is to the next character in the message. You should now be able to put together a simple program fragment which given a pointer to a message will print the message character by character until a zero-valued element is encountered.

One version appears as follows:

while (*param1 != '\0')

```
{

        putchar(*param1);

        param1++;

}
```

[handwritten margin notes: for (a; b; c) statement; a: while (b) { statement c; }]

The operation of this example is quite simple to appreciate. The next version of the same thing is more complex to read but it should generate more efficient code when compiled:

for (; *param1; putchar(*param1++));

Obviously, this is a **for** loop. Notice first that the controlled statement is empty. This is shown by the semicolon which immediately follows the **for** brackets (make a mental note at this point not to put a semicolon here by accident because it is not a syntax error and so the compiler will not point it out to you). The second thing to note is that there is no initialization expression inside the **for** brackets before the first semicolon. This is fine as there is no initialization to perform in this case. The third point is that the termination condition has changed. When you are only considering whether an expression is TRUE (non-zero) or FALSE (zero) then even though the numeric result might be different, the expressions:

*param1 != '\0'

and

*param1

are always TRUE at the same time and FALSE at the same time and so can be used interchangeably in construct condition expressions. If you are not convinced, try out a few different values for yourself. The final point to look at concerns that rather strange incremental expression:

putchar(*param1++)

The first thing that happens here is that the **putchar** parameter is evaluated so that its value can be passed to **putchar** later. The parameter is:

*param1++

Looking up the two operators in Table 8.1 shows that they are both unary operators with the same precedence level so that they are evaluated right to left as shown by the associativity. This means that the expression is equivalent to:

*(param1++)

so that the **++** operator is evaluated first. Notice, however, that as the **++** follows **param1** it means post-increment. The implied bracket therefore returns the current value of **param1** and then **param1** is incremented. So it is the address in **param1** before it is incremented that is acted on by the asterisk (*) operator. This yields the character pointed at by **param1** as the overall value and **param1** is then incremented ready for next time round.

As an aside try to work out the operation of the following code fragment which uses a similar expression to the above but forces execution of the unary asterisk (*) operator first:

*param1='a';

putchar((*param1)++);

Obviously the first line assigns the character value 'a' to the memory location pointed to by **param1**. The value of **param1** will previously need to have been set to point to a **char** variable. On the next line evaluation of the **putchar** parameter takes place first. That is evaluation of:

(*param1)++

The brackets are evaluated first to give the character value 'a' that **param1** is pointing at. When the increment (++) operator is applied to the value 'a' it will give the value 'b' but notice that it is a post-increment that will not be performed until after the value 'a' has been used. The effect of this line then is to print the character value 'a' and then increment the contents of the memory location pointed to by **param1** from 'a' to 'b'.

In the case of consecutive **char** values in memory it is obvious that a **char** pointer needs to be incremented by one to move from one character to the next. In fact the same thing is arranged to be true for variables of any kind. So that if a list of **int** values for example is arranged to occupy consecutive locations in memory then an **int** pointer can be made to point to the first **int** in the list. If the pointer is subsequently incremented it will not have just 1 added to it because this would leave it pointing somewhere inside the first **int** value. Instead it will automatically be incremented by the size of an **int** value (or whatever else it is pointing to). It is in order to get pointer arithmetic right that the compiler needs to be told what type of object a pointer is pointing at. With this information the compiler can arrange to add the right amount to a pointer when it is incremented. So if **pi** is declared to be an **int** pointer, that is set up to point to the start of a list of consecutive **int** values then:

*pi   **is the first value**

*(pi+1)   **is the second value**

*(pi+2)   **is the third value**

and so on, remembering that when an integer value is added to a pointer, the value is automatically scaled by the size of what the pointer points at.

11.6 POINTERS AND ARRAYS

It is about now that you should be able to see why pointers and arrays are treated together in the same chapter.

Consider the following declarations and assignment:

int table[10],*pi;

pi = &table[0];

Here an **int** array called **table** is declared to be 10 elements long and an **int** pointer is also declared called **pi**. Then **pi** is assigned the address of the first element of the array.

After this has been done you should be able to see that:

*pi or ***(pi+0)** is the same as **table[0]**
    and ***(pi+1)** is the same as **table[1]**
    and ***(pi+2)** is the same as **table[2]**
and so on right down to
        *(pi+9) is the same as **table[9]**

As you can see, a direct correspondence exists between accessing the values with a pointer and accessing them as an array.

In fact there is an even closer correspondence than appears at first sight. Finding the address of the first element of an array is such a common thing to do that C is arranged so that when the name of an array is used as a term in an expression it automatically returns the address of the first element in the array as its value. This means that instead of:

pi = &table[0];

you could just write:

pi = table;

But the same rule also has more subtle consequences like:

table[6]

is exactly equivalent to:

*(table+6)

because **table** is a pointer to the start of the array.

The same argument also works in reverse, so that where you write:

*(pi+5)

in an expression, with **pi** declared as an **int** pointer, it is also acceptable to write:

pi[5]

There is, however, one difference between the two values **pi** and **table**. They are both pointers, but **pi** is a pointer variable whereas **table** is a pointer constant. This means that **pi** has memory space allocated to holding its value, allowing constructs like:

pi++;

or

pi = table;

to be used. However, no memory is used at run time to hold the value of **table**; it is just something that the compiler knows about at compile time. Consequently it makes no sense to use expressions like:

table++;

or

table = pi;

because this implies moving the array from the place allocated to it by the compiler to some other position in memory which clearly cannot be allowed.

Now you have seen the connection between arrays, strings and pointers you should be able to understand how the following example works:

char *message;

message = "Hello, world\n";

printf(message);

Here, **message** is declared as a pointer to **char**. You remember that a string literal evaluates to a pointer to its first character and that the string is automatically zero terminated. The second line therefore causes the storage of the text "Hello, world\n" in memory and the return of a pointer to this text, which is then assigned to the pointer variable **message**. The third line is a **printf** function call, whose parameter is normally a string literal. However, since this just evaluates to a pointer to the string then using the value of a pointer variable instead is equally acceptable. This then is a roundabout way to print the message "Hello, world".

Notice in the second line of the above example that there is no string copying going on. All that is happening here is that a pointer to a text message is being assigned to a pointer variable called **message**. String copying is more complex than just a simple assignment and has to be performed one character at a time.

11.7 INITIALIZING char ARRAYS

You have already seen how to initialize a static or external array with **int** elements and indeed a **char** array can be initialized in the same way and under the same circumstances. But very often you will want to initialize a **char** array with a string value and that is a bit tedious using the standard method:

static char message[] = {'w','o','r','d','\0'};

To overcome this problem **char** arrays can be initialized with string values in a shorthand way as follows:

static char message[] = "word";

just using a string literal in double quotes instead of all the character constants, commas and brackets.

11.8 STRING FUNCTIONS

Where string copying is necessary, a simple function to perform the operation might be:

```
strcpy(s1,s2)
char *s1,*s2;
{
        while (*s1++ = *s2++);
}
```

This function will copy a zero-terminated string pointed to by parameter **s2** into a **char** array pointed to by **s1**. As you can see, the function is very compact consisting of only a single line. It requires a lot of understanding of C expressions to make this line work but you should have all the required knowledge by now so here goes.

Obviously this is a **while** loop whose controlled statement is empty, as you can see by the semicolon on the end of the line. The **while** construct is a looping statement that will continue to iterate until its conditional expression evaluates to 0 (FALSE). The conditional expression in this case is:

*s1++ = *s2++

Inserting the brackets that are implied by operator precedence and associativity gives:

(*(s1++)) = (*(s2++))

Working on the right-hand side of the assignment operator first gives:

*(s2++)

which you have seen in a similar example previously. It evaluates to whatever **s2** is currently pointing at and then it also increments **s2** for next time round. Moving over to the left of the assignment now, you can see that this value that has emerged from the right-hand side is to be assigned to the location that **s1** is pointing at and then **s1** will be post-incremented ready for next time round. So on each iteration round the loop, the location pointed to by **s2** is copied to the location pointed to by **s1** then **s2** and **s1** are both incremented. Finally, remember that the assignment operators return the value that is assigned to the variable on the left as their result and that this value is the value of the conditional expression in this example. Iteration will therefore continue until the value returned (i.e. the character copied) is a 0 and this only happens at the end of the string as required.

There is no reason why you should not write a whole set of string manipulation functions to concatenate, copy and compare strings. They are all fairly simple functions that are each only a few lines long. However, the labour is unnecessary as they are all provided as standard functions.

All you have to do is to add the following line at the start of your programs:

#include <string.h>

and the following string functions become available.

11.8.1 Concatenate

char *strcat(s1,s2)

char *s1,*s2;

As you can see, the function **strcat** returns a value that is a **char** pointer and also takes two parameters both of which are **char** pointers. Parameters

s1 and **s2** should both point to **char** arrays. Function **strcat** glues both of the strings together into one string, taking the **s1** string first and following it with the **s2** string. The zero terminator at the end of string 1 is removed so that the result is just a single string. The resulting string is built up in the array pointed to by **s1** so this array must be large enough to hold the result and not just string 1. The value returned by **strcat** is just the value of parameter **s1**.

11.8.2 Copy

char *strcpy(s1,s2)

char *s1,*s2;

The **strcpy** function performs just the same job as the example you studied earlier except that a pointer value is returned. It is just the value of parameter **s1**.

11.8.3 Compare

int strcmp(s1,s2)

char *s2,*s2;

The string compare function **strcmp** compares the strings pointed to by **s1** and **s2** character by character until a difference is found between the two strings or the end of the strings is reached. The return value from **strcmp** is an **int** with value 0 if string 1 is equal to string 2 (i.e. the end of both strings is reached with no differences found), a negative value if string 1 is alphabetically earlier than string 2 or a positive value if string 1 is alphabetically later then string 2. Earlier and later in this context means before and after in the order of the underlying character code.

11.9 ARRAYS OF POINTERS

To finish off the chapter I shall cover a point which is most useful, the idea of an array of pointers. You may be forgiven at this point in time if you do not see an obvious use for this data structure but consider it further.

Suppose you wish to work with the names of the days of the week and that you would like to write a function which, given a day number in the range 0–6, would return a pointer to a string containing the day name. Such a function might be:

```
char *dayname(d)
int d;
{
        char *dayptr[7];

        dayptr[0] = "Sunday";
        dayptr[1] = "Monday";
        dayptr[2] = "Tuesday";
        dayptr[3] = "Wednesday";
        dayptr[4] = "Thursday";
        dayptr[5] = "Friday";
        dayptr[6] = "Saturday";

        return(dayptr[d]);
}
```

Here, the function **dayname** is declared to return a value of type **char** pointer as required and to take a single integer parameter, **d** representing the day number whose name needs to be returned. Inside the function body an array is declared called **dayptr** which is seven elements long. Each element is declared to be of type **char** pointer. Then, each of the seven pointers in the array is initialized to point to one of the seven day names "Sunday" to "Saturday". Finally, the value of the parameter (**d**) is used to select one of the seven pointers as the function's return value.

As written, this function works well; however, there is an unnecessary overhead of having to set up the pointer values in the array each time the function is called. Just as it is possible to initialize ordinary static and external arrays it is also possible to initialize arrays of pointers as long as they too are static or external.

A second and more efficient version of the same function which illustrates this initialization process is as follows:

```
char *dayname(d)
int d;
{
        static char *dayptr[] =
        {
                "Sunday",
                "Monday",
                "Tuesday",
                "Wednesday",
                "Thursday",
                "Friday",
                "Saturday"
        };

        return(dayptr[d]);
}
```

Notice that the compiler does not need to be given an explicit size for the **dayptr** array; the number of elements can be counted from the number of initialization strings. This is a much more efficient solution than the first because the **dayptr** array values are set up during the compilation process in this second version rather than at run time.

11.10 POINTERS TO POINTERS

Remember that because **dayptr** in the above example is an array that the name **dayptr** itself is a pointer constant to the first element of the array. This would allow the following code fragment:

char **pp;

pp = dayptr;

The variable **pp** is declared to be a pointer which points to pointers which point to **char**. And just from the make-up of the **dayptr** array you know this to be the case.

This single variable value (**pp**) can now be passed to any function, where it can be used to access any of the strings underneath, which in this example are each days of the week. For example, to use **pp** to print the string "Wednesday" requires only a line like:

printf(pp[3]);

This may seem complex but a simple diagram should clear things up a bit (see Fig. 11.1).

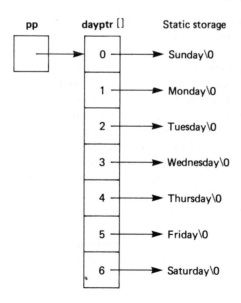

Fig. 11.1 pp is a pointer to an array of pointers to char arrays

You already know that:

pp+1

will add on to the value of **pp** the size of whatever it is pointing at.

Since **pp** points at **dayptr[0]** then
      pp+1 points at **dayptr[1]** and so on
Now,**pp+3** points at **dayptr[3]**
and   ***(pp+3)** is what **pp+3** points at
so   ***(pp+3)** is equal to **dayptr[3]**
but   ***(pp+3)** is also equal to **pp[3]**
so   **pp[3]** is equal to **dayptr[3]**
and   **dayptr[3]** is a pointer to the string "Wednesday" as required

11.10.1 Passing parameters to main ()

This unusual trick of passing a single pointer to give access to several lines of text is used quite a lot in C and in one special case in particular.

There have been several occasions when you have run a command under control of the UNIX shell and passed extra parameters into the command such as flags to direct its operation or file names for it to operate on. For example:

$ ls −l

$ wc /etc/passwd

Somehow the commands must be able to pick up these extra parameters on the command line and use them internally.

What happens is as follows: the individual words on the command line including the command name itself are split up and stored in separate arrays of characters. A pointer is then set up to point to the start of each of the separate strings and the whole set of pointers is stored in an array just as you have already seen. Finally, a pointer to the start of this array is passed as a parameter into the function **main** so that all you need do is to declare a parameter variable in **main** to receive the value and then you can access the command line parameters. There is one further slight complication to this scheme which you will soon realize is a necessity. As well as passing a pointer to the command line text strings, an integer value is also passed into **main** which specifies how many separate strings there are available from the command line.

As an example, here is a simple command which will examine all the words following the name on the command line, looking for a consecutive pair that are the same. I leave you to sort out its operation:

```
#include <stdio.h>
#include <string.h>

main(argc,argv)
int argc;                 /* number of parameters */
char **argv;              /* pointer to array of pointers */
{
        int f = 1;

        while (--argc)
        {
                ++argv;
                if (!strcmp(*argv,*(argv+1)))
                {
                        printf("I found a match\n");
                        f = 0;
                }
        }

        if (f)
                printf("No match found");
}
```

As you can see, **main** has been declared with two parameter variables. The first is traditionally called **argc** which is an **int** and a count of the number of strings into which the command line was split. Remember that the command name itself also counts as one. The second parameter is traditionally called **argv** which is declared as a pointer to a pointer to **char**.

char **argv;

Due to the equivalence of pointers and arrays that you have seen you will also find **argv** declared sometimes as an array of pointers as follows:

char *argv[];

These two declarations are exactly equivalent and can be used interchangeably.

Input and output

So far the only input and output you have seen has been via the standard input and output devices using the functions **getchar** for input and **putchar** and **printf** for output. In this chapter you will discover that input to and output from C programs is much more powerful than you have used yet.

12.1 FORMATTED OUTPUT

I shall start this section with a full and proper treatment of **printf**. Up to now you have seen two examples of its use. One to print out strings:

printf("Hello, world\n");

and the other to print out decimal integer values:

printf("%d",num);

In fact these are just two specific examples of a much more powerful and flexible system. In its most general form, **printf** can be used to print out any sorts of values in any number and in any order and to format the values printed on output. Formatting the values means that you can choose how numeric values are printed (decimal, octal, hexadecimal, floating point or scientific notation) and how wide a field will be used to contain each item printed.

The whole power of the **printf** function is based on the idea of using a control string which specifies the number and types of values to be printed. The general form of the **printf** function call is:

printf("Control string", param2, param3, . . .);

Notice that the first parameter is always the control string but as you saw in Chapter 11 this need not be a string literal. In its simplest form the control string can be the only parameter passed to **printf**. The string:

printf("Hello, world\n");

is an example of this. Where the values of general expressions are to be printed these have to be specified as extra parameters. To tell the **printf** function that more parameters follow the control string, special expression type and format codes are embedded within the control string itself. These codes always begin with a per cent sign (%). There will be one per cent sign for each extra parameter expression in the **printf** call.

The ordinary characters to be printed and the format specifications can be freely mixed within the control string. For example:

printf("Value x=%d and y=%d\n",x,y);

Here the control string is:

"Value x=%d and y=%d\n"

Notice that there are two format specifications starting with per cent signs within the control string. This means that there must be two extra parameter expressions following the control string, separated by commas. And indeed there are, in this example they are just the variables **x** and **y**. Following the per cent signs is some information to specify what type of value to expect the corresponding extra parameter expressions to yield and also how to format the values for printing. In the example both per cent signs are followed by the format specification '**d**' which tells **printf** to expect signed integer values from the corresponding parameter expressions and to print the values in decimal. When the control string is printed, the **%d** specification will be replaced by the values of the corresponding extra parameter expressions. If **x = 6** and **y = 12** then the above example would print the line:

Value x=6 and y=12

This method allows all sorts of values to be embedded within normal text output. You can now see how the **printf** line you have been using for printing integer variable values works:

printf("%d",num);

The **%d** specification is not the only one available, the complete list is:

d	The parameter is treated as a signed integer value that is printed in decimal
u	The parameter is treated as an unsigned integer value again printed in decimal
x	The parameter is treated as an unsigned integer value but now printed in hexadecimal (base 16)
o	Same as **x** but the value is printed in octal (base 8)
e	The parameter is treated as **float** or **double** which is printed in decimal in exponential or scientific notation (i.e. [−]i.dddddde[±]nn)
f	Same as **e** but printed in a more conventional format (i.e. [−]iii.dddddd)
g	Evaluates a **float** or **double** as for **e** and **f** and then prints out whichever generates the shorter string

c   The parameter is taken to be a single character
s   The parameter is taken to be a string (i.e. a pointer to a zero-terminated **char** array)

In between the per cent sign and the format specification character there may also be further information giving a more detailed specification. A string of digits will specify the minimum field width in which the value will be printed. If the value occupies less space than specified then the value will be padded on the left with spaces up to the specified field width. In the case of integer values if the first digit of the field width specifier is a zero then the value will be padded on the left with zeros rather than spaces. And if the string of digits is preceded by a minus (−) sign then the space padding will be added to the right instead of the left.

In some cases a second extra specification may also be given as well as or instead of the first. This consists of a full stop (.) followed by another digit string. In the case of **float** or **double** values this gives the number of digits to print after the decimal point. And in the case of strings it specifies the maximum number of characters that will be printed from the string whatever its length.

Finally in cases where **int** and **long** are different sizes it is also possible for format specification characters **d**, **u**, **x** and **o** to be directly preceded by the letter **l** where **long** is intended.

Some example format specifications and their effects are illustrated below:

```
printf("!%6d!\n",123)            gives    !   123!
printf("!%-6d!\n",456)           gives    !456   !
printf("!%06d!\n",789)           gives    !000789!
printf("!%2x!\n",205)            gives    !cd!
printf("!%2X!\n",205)            gives    !CD!
printf("!%2x!\n",12)             gives    ! c!
printf("!%02x!\n",12)            gives    !0c!
printf("!%10.2e!\n",123.456)     gives    !  1.23e+02!
printf("!%10.3E!\n",123.456)     gives    ! 1.235E+02!
printf("!%10s!\n","string")      gives    !    string!
printf("!%-10s!\n","string")     gives    !string    !
printf("!%10.4s!\n","string")    gives    !      stri!
printf("!%lu!\n,12345L)          gives    !12345!
```

12.2 FORMATTED INPUT

As you can see, the **printf** function provides general facilities for formatting and printing values. As yet you have only seen the **getchar** function for taking input into a program. There is, however, a much more powerful function in the standard library which provides the same sort of facilities on input that **printf** provides on output. The name of this new function is **scanf**. The general form of the **scanf** function call is similar to **printf**:

scanf("control string", param2, param3, . . .);

Again this function is control-string driven and again the control string specifies with per cent signs the number of extra parameters after itself. Remember that the task that **scanf** will be required to perform is that it should take values as input that follow some specified format and assign the values to variables of an appropriate type within the current function. Where more than one value will be read by a single **scanf** call, the individual values on input should be separated by white space characters ('\t', '\n' or space). You already know that parameters are only passed to functions by value so that if **scanf** is to alter variable values within the current function then it will need to be passed pointers to the variables to change. You should not be surprised to find therefore that all the extra parameters that appear after the control string in a **scanf** call need to be pointers to variables of the required types.

As with **printf**, the **scanf** format specifications are per cent signs followed by single letters. These are:

d	An integer value is expected, entered as a decimal number
x	As for **d** but expects value in hexadecimal
o	As for **d** but expects value in octal
h	A **short** value is expected, entered as a decimal number
f	A **float** value is expected
c	Expects a single character. Normally a white space character is used to terminate a field to a **scanf** call but for %c a white space character will be treated like any other character that might be received
s	Expects a white space terminated character string. The corresponding extra parameter should be a pointer to the start of a **char** array that is large enough to take the string and a '\0' terminator that will be added automatically

The **scanf** function also allows you to specify a digit string between the per cent sign and the format specification character, which will be taken as the maximum number of characters to be accepted for the particular field.

The format specifications **d**, **x**, **o** and **f** may also be directly preceded by a letter **l** which indicates that the pointers to **long** and **double** variables should be used instead of **int** and **float** respectively.

Assuming the existence of a set of variables declared as follows:

```
char str[20];
int a,b,c;
double d;
```

Then the following are valid examples of the use of **scanf**:

```
scanf("%2d%3d%2d", &a,&b,&c);
```
with input 1234567
assigns a=12, b=345, c=67

scanf ("%x%lf%s", &a,&d,str);
with input 2cab 12.2E7 Jones
assigns a=0x2cab d=12.2E7

and the first six elements of str[] are set to 'J', 'o', 'n', 'e', 's', '\0' respectively.

12.3 FILE I/O

Even with the full versions of **printf** and **scanf** you have still only seen input from and output to the standard I/O devices. Using the shell to redirect input and output you have seen how to take input from and send output to disc files. These techniques are fine for small utility programs with simple I/O requirements, but what do you do when a program needs to access the data in a file out of sequence or if more than one input file or output file is required?

Obviously, there has to be a way to access files directly to cope with these situations and indeed there is.

Remember that all input and output through UNIX is via files. Before any file can be used it has to be connected to the program. In the case of the standard input and output files they are automatically connected to your programs by the shell before your programs are run. To connect your own files to your programs you need to use a system library function called **fopen**. Generally input and output data is held in a buffer that is inserted in between your file reading and writing operations and actual read and write operations to disc data blocks. This buffering is to improve disc access efficiency. However, this means that when you write information to go to a disc file, the function you call has actually to write the data to the buffer. Similarly when you read information from a file, the function you call actually reads the data from the buffer. Only when the buffer is full on writing data or empty on reading data will a request be made to access the disc copy of the file. Obviously before you can access a file a data buffer needs to be allocated to the file for data buffering and some other supervisory operations. This is the job of the **fopen** library function. You supply as parameters to **fopen** the name of the file and information on how you would like to be able to access the file (reading, writing, appending, etc.) and **fopen** returns as its value a pointer to the buffer that has been allocated for I/O operations to the specified file, or a NULL value (NULL is a zero-valued pointer) if an error occurred and a buffer could not be allocated. (If, for example, you do not have permission to access the file!)

The format for the **fopen** call is:

fp = fopen(filename, type);

Notice that the value returned by **fopen** is saved for future use in a variable, here **fp**. You will appreciate the wisdom of this action later. One problem arising is that as the function returns a type other than **int** it needs to be declared before it is used. What type should it be declared as? Well, whatever type it is the variable **fp** needs to be declared as the same type because it receives the value returned by the **fopen** call. The actual type is system-dependent because the value is a pointer to a buffer and the buffer structure can be different on different systems. To save you knowing what the structure looks like the proper type is defined in **stdio.h** and given the name FILE (notice the capital letters).

Using FILE the variable **fp** and the return type of **fopen** just require a declaration like the following:

FILE *fp, *fopen();

where FILE is treated just like any other basic data type.

The file name parameter in the example **fopen** call is just a pointer to a **char** array containing the file name string or of course a file name string literal within double quotes.

The type parameter is also a pointer to a string that specifies the type of access to the file that will be allowed.

Acceptable values of type are:

r	Opens a file for read only. Reading starts at the beginning of the file. It is an error to try to read a file that does not exist
w	Creates an empty file for write only. If the specified file already exists then its contents are deleted before writing begins
a	Opens an existing file for write only. The write operations commence at the end of the file's existing contents so that the new data is appended to the existing. If the specified file does not exist then this option is the same as **w**
r+	Opens an existing file for read and write operations from the start of the file
w+	Creates a new file or deletes the contents of an existing file and opens the file for read and write
a+	Opens an existing file for read and write operations beginning at the end of the existing data

The values above that use the plus (+) sign can be used for both read and write operations on the same file provided that either an **fseek** or **rewind** function call is used or an EOF is detected between a read and a write or a write and a read operation (**fseek** and **rewind** will be covered soon).

Having opened a file and been allocated a buffer, a pointer (usually called a **file** pointer) is returned to specify where the associated buffer is located. On subsequent calls to any standard functions that will be used to access or alter the buffer contents the function will need to know where the buffer is, so that its data may be changed. To achieve this the saved value of the file pointer returned by **fopen** should be passed as a parameter to all the function calls that will access this file.

For each of the input and output functions you have seen so far that operate on the standard I/O devices, there is a corresponding general purpose I/O function that will operate in the same way except that a file pointer needs to be specified as a parameter in addition to any other parameters.

So the **getchar** and **putchar** functions become:

c = getc(fp);
putc(c,fp);

The **getc** function takes a file pointer as a parameter and returns the next character from the associated file which then is assigned to **c**. Just as with **getchar** an EOF condition is returned when the end of the file is reached.

The **putc** function takes two parameters. The first is the character value to send to the file and the second is a file pointer for the required file. The **putc** function returns an **int** value that is equal to the parameter **c** if all goes well, or EOF if the function fails for any reason.

Because all UNIX I/O is via files even the standard I/O devices you have used so often must have file pointers associated with them — and indeed they have. These file pointers are set up by the shell when the standard I/O devices are opened. Special names are given to the standard file pointers. They are:

stdin   Standard input file pointer
stdout   Standard output file pointer
stderr   Standard error output file pointer

Without I/O redirection the **stdin** device is the keyboard and the **stdout** and **stderr** devices are both connected to your terminal screen. The reason for **stderr** is so that the error messages can still be sent to your screen even if **stdout** has been redirected.

Once you have the file pointers for the standard I/O devices then these devices can be accessed with **getc** and **putc** just like any other file. In fact if you enter the command:

$ cat </usr/include/stdio.h

which is the file you #**include** in your C programs, you will find that there are #**defines** for **getchar** and **putchar** in terms of **getc**, **putc**, **stdin** and **stdout** as follows:

#define getchar() getc(stdin)
#define putchar(c) putc(c,stdout)

This means that you have been using file pointers and proper file I/O all along but the system kept it hidden from you.

12.4 FORMATTED FILE I/O

The file I/O equivalents to **printf** and **scanf** are called:

fprintf(fp, "control string", extra params . . .)
fscanf (fp,"control string", extra params . . .)

These are identical to their standard I/O cousins except for the addition of the file pointer before the control string.

As an aside, sometimes you have a variable value that you want to convert into a string of characters but not for printing or storing in a file. In effect what you need is a version of **printf** or **fprintf** but which will send its output to a **char** array.

In fact, there are string versions of both **printf** and **scanf** in C called:

sprintf(str,"control string", extra params . . .)
sscanf(stf,"control string", extra params . . .)

where **str** is just a pointer to a **char** array.

12.5 CODING A 'MORE' COMMAND

Now that you have seen how to take parameters into a program from the command line and how to perform direct file I/O you should be able to write a simple version of **more** as described in Chapter 2 (particularly useful if your system does not provide it).

One possible solution might be:

```c
#include <stdio.h>

main(argc,argv)
int·argc;
char *argv[];
{
        FILE *fp, *fopen();
        int i,lincnt,c;

        for (i=1; i<argc; i++)
        {
                lincnt = 0;
                if ((fp = fopen(argv[i],"r")) == NULL)
                        fprintf(stderr,"Error with file %s\n",argv[i]);
                else
                {
                        fprintf(stderr,"Listing file %s\n",argv[i]);
                        while ((c = getchar()) != '\n');
                        while ((c = getc(fp)) != EOF)
                        {
                                if (c == '\n')
                                        lincnt++;

                                if (lincnt != 22)
                                        putchar(c);
                                else
                                {
                                        while ((c = getchar()) != '\n');
                                        lincnt = 0;
                                }
                        }
                        fclose(fp);
                }
        }
}
```

This is a rather simplified version of the usual **more** command, it just accepts **return** to list the next page. It is called as follows:

$ **more filenames**

This assumes that you call the command **more** when you compile it. The command itself does introduce one idea that is new to you. It will allow more than one file to be specified on the command line. All of the files will be listed one after the other as though **more** had been called for each file in turn. Obviously by this method you could specify any arbitrary number of files to be listed. Each file specified will be **fopen**ed in turn and printed. Because only a limited number of file buffers are available to any particular command process (20 is the standard number) after this number of files have been opened further **fopen** calls will fail unless steps are taken to overcome this problem. After each file has been printed in the **more** application, its file buffer is no longer required and so the best solution would be to return the buffer to the free pool so that it may be used again. A standard function to do this job in C is:

fclose(fp);

The **fclose** function takes as its parameter the file pointer to the buffer to be returned to the pool. As you can see, **fclose** has been included in the example **more** listing at the end of the printing loop.

It should also be pointed out at this time that because the program has been written to accept multiple files on the command line it will also automatically accept command lines like:

$ **more *.c**

That is, command lines that involve the use of ambiguous file names. As you already know, these ambiguous file names are dealt with by the UNIX shell which will evaluate and expand them and pass the expanded version as a set of parameters into your programs.

12.6 RANDOM ACCESS FILES

All the file access you have seen so far has been sequential access in that, when reading data for example, you have started at the beginning of the file and read each character in the file in turn until EOF is encountered.

In some situations this is either not sufficient or would lead to very inefficient programs. In these cases what is needed is a way to specify where within the file the next read or write operation should take place.

The simplest operation is just to go back to the start of the file and resume sequential read and write operations from there. This would allow multiple passes to be made through a disc file, and can be achieved with the standard function:

rewind(fp);

You can think of this operation almost like rewinding the tape on a tape recorder so that a particular piece of music may be replayed.

In situations where a particular position within the file needs to be reached then the **rewind** function is still not sufficient and a new function is needed called:

fseek(fp,offset,base)
FILE *fp;
long offset;
int base;

Notice the types of the three parameters. The first (**fp**) is just the file pointer for the relevant file. The second (**offset**) is declared to be a **long**. This is because this value specifies the number of bytes into the file that the next read or write should take place, and a 16-bit value here would not allow for files longer than 64K. The third parameter (**base**) is an **int** and specifies what the second parameter is offset from. If **base** is 0 then the **offset** is the number of bytes from the start of the file. If the **base** is 1 then the **offset** is added to the current position in the file. And if **base** is 2 then the **offset** is from the end of the file.

If for any reason you need to know what the current offset value is, measured from the start of the file, then this can be discovered with the function call:

l = ftell(fp);

Do not forget that the file offsets are **long**, so **ftell** will return a **long**. This means a declaration like the following will be required before **ftell** is used:

long l,ftell();

13 | Structures and unions

The only method of organizing a collection of data items that you have seen so far has been via the use of an array. The array structure is fine if all the elements in it are of the same type. But what do you do if you want to collect together a general record of information, like an entry from a phone book or an order line on an invoice where each of the different fields within the record is of a different size or type?

13.1 STRUCTURES

In C the answer is to use a structure. A structure is just a collection of data items of any required types that can be referred to collectively by a single name.

The general format for a structure declaration is:

struct tag-name
{
      variable-declaration
      variable-declaration

      _____

      _____

}
variable-name-list;

The declaration begins with the word **struct**. Following this is an item called the **tag-name**. In fact this item is optional, but if it is supplied it has the same syntax as all other C identifier names. As you will see later in this chapter the **tag** allows a shorthand way to refer to the structure layout when you wish to declare variables with this structure at several different places in the program. Think of it as though specifying a **tag-name** for a structure was like setting up a template to aid future declarations of structure variables with this structure layout.

Within the curly brackets are a set of variable declarations that define the types and names of the individual fields within the structure. These variable declarations have exactly the same form as those you are familiar with already.

After the curly brackets a list of variable names may follow. This list is optional but if supplied will declare a set of variables with the given internal structure. Notice that the variable name list is terminated by a semicolon. This semicolon must be present even if you opt not to supply the variable name list.

A typical structure declaration for an invoice order line might be:

```
struct
{
        char      transtype,
                  description[50];
        int       qty;
        float     price,
                  value,
                  vat,
                  total;
}
line;
```

This declares a structure variable called **line** which has an internal structure consisting of seven individual fields. The first field is a single **char** value to store information about the transaction type (sale, loan, exchange, etc.). The second field is a **char** array of 50 characters that will be used to hold the description of the product of this record. Field three is an **int** specifying the quantity involved and the last four fields are all of type **float** as they involve amounts of money.

In situations where variables with this structure will be used and declared in several places it is better to declare a **tag-name** and then declare the structure variables with the **tag**:

```
struct invline
{
        char      transtype,
                  description[50];
        int       qty;
        float     price,
                  value,
                  vat,
                  total;
};
```

Essentially this structure template has been given the name **invline** and variables with this structure can now be declared using this **tag** as follows:

struct invline line;

This declares **line** to have the above structure just as in the previous example where line was declared directly.

You now have a variable available whose value is the entire record of information declared in the structure and whose name is **line**. This is fine, but obviously at some point you will need to be able to access the individual elements within the structure so as to be able to assign values to them and perform computations using them, just like ordinary variables. This is where one of the two operators comes into the picture that you have yet to meet. It is the dot (.) operator or structure member operator.

To access an individual field within a structure all you need to do is to give the structure name followed by the element name separated by a dot:

line.qty

is the quantity element within the **line** structure. As **qty** is declared to be of type **int** then **line.qty** is also an **int**. This means it can be used in any situation where an ordinary **int** variable can be used:

line.qty=16;
printf("Quantity=%d\n",line.qty);
line.qty--;

and so on. In standard C there are very few operations that can be performed on a structure as a whole. In fact there are just two operations. You can take individual elements and manipulate them as you have just seen or you can set up a pointer to point to the start of a structure and then access the structure elements with the pointer instead of the structure variable name. This works because a structure pointer is just the address in memory of the structures first element.

This allows constructs like:

```
struct invline line, *linptr;

linptr = & line;
(*linptr).qty = 10;
printf("Total=%f\n",(*linptr).total);
```

What this example shows is the declaration of a structure variable called **line** and the declaration of a pointer to a structure called **linptr**. Both of these variables refer to a structure with the template **invline** you have seen before.

Having declared the variables, **linptr** is set up to point to the structure **line** and the pointer is then used to access elements within the structure using the dot (.) operator as before. Notice in using the structure pointer the inclusion of brackets around the asterisk and the pointer name. These are necessary because the structure member operator, dot, has a higher precedence than the pointer operator and would otherwise be evaluated first giving the wrong result.

This idea of using a pointer to access structure members is such a common construct in C that a special notation is available that uses the last one of the operators from Chapter 8. The operator is the structure pointer operator $(->)$ and in use it appears as:

linptr−>qty = 10;

This is exactly equivalent to the notation:

(*linptr).qty = 10;

except that it is much easier to read and much clearer as to its meaning.

In standard C these are all the operations that can be performed on a structure. Specifically they cannot be assigned one to another except one element at a time, and they cannot be passed as parameters to functions or returned by a function as its result. However, under UNIX system V all of these extras have been added to the C compiler so that programs like the following trivial example can run:

```
#include <stdio.h>

struct example
{
        int a,b;
};
main()
{
        struct example var1,var2;

        var1.a = 10;
        var1.b = 20;

        var2 = var1;

        printf("a=%d b=%d\n",var2.a,var2.b);
}
```

This shows that in the assignment:

var2 = var1;

all of the elements of **var1** were copied into the corresponding elements in **var2**.

13.2 INITIALIZING STRUCTURE ELEMENTS

Again, just as with arrays, an external or static structure can have the values of its elements initialized when it is declared. The syntax for this is very similar to the array case:

```
struct invline line =
{
        's',              /* transtype */
        "ACETYLENE",      /* description */
        1,                /* quantity */
        97.76,            /* price */
        97.76,            /* value */
        14.66             /* tax */
        112.42            /* total */
};
```

Notice that individual element initializers are separated by commas and all enclosed in curly brackets. All you have to make sure of is that each initializer given is of the right type to match the corresponding structure element.

13.3 GROWING TREES

One particularly valuable use for structures is to form the building blocks from which more complex data structures can be made. Examples are linked lists, queues, stacks and trees. The reason why structures are so well suited to these applications is that the individual elements of each of these data constructs contain a pointer or pointers to other elements in the data construct as well as the data itself.

Consider a simple linked list, each element in the list consisting of two parts. The first part is the information content of the element and the second part is a pointer that points to the next element in the list.

The individual elements can easily be modelled with a structure as follows:

struct element
{
     int value;
     struct element *link;
};

This shows a structure with tag-name element to consist of an **int** part called **value** and a second part that is a pointer called **link** to another structure of type element (see Fig. 13.1).

Using these **link** pointers individual elements can be connected together to form the required linked list (see Fig. 13.2). As an example, functions to find the length of the list and to search for the presence or absence of an element containing a particular value are easy to write. These solutions assume that the elements in the list are not ordered in any particular way, and that a global variable exists called **start** that is a pointer to the first element in the list. I shall also assume that the last element contains a NULL value as its **link** pointer (see Fig. 13.3).

Fig. 13.1 Layout of a structure called element

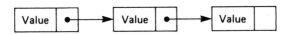

Fig. 13.2 Several element structures linked

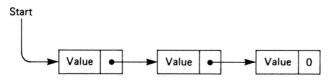

Fig. 13.3 Linked elements with start pointer and a NULL end pointer.

```
listlen()
{
        struct element *ptr;
        int count;

        ptr = start;

        for (count = 0; ptr != NULL; count++)
                ptr = ptr->link;

        return(count);
}
```

This function declares a working pointer to an element (**ptr**) which is initialized to point to the start of the list. While the value of **ptr** is not NULL (i.e. while this is not the last element) move the pointer one element further into the list and increment the **count** by 1.

```
findval(data)
int data;
{
        struct element *ptr;
        int found;

        ptr = start;

        for (found = 0; ptr != NULL; ptr = ptr->link)
                if (ptr->value == data)
                        found = 1;

        return(found);
```

Here a similar tour to the last example is made through the linked list, but this time the data value in each element is compared with the value of the parameter passed to the function. A flag variable called **found** is initially set to 0 but this is changed to 1 if a match is found in any of the comparisons. At the end of the loop the value of variable **found** is returned as the result of the function. Consequently **findval** returns a 0 if the required value is not found in the linked list or 1 if it is.

Notice that there is some inefficiency in this second function because the linked list will be searched to the end (NULL value) even if the required data value is encountered in the first element. This problem is easily overcome by adding a **break** statement inside the **for** loop to terminate it early if the required value is found:

```
for (found = 0; ptr != NULL; ptr = ptr->link)
        if (ptr->value == data)
        {
                found = 1;
                break;
        }

return(found);
```

As an exercise, think up another solution to the same problem but without the use of **break**.

Once linked lists are mastered it is only a short step to adding another link pointer into the element structure in order to allow the building of trees:

```
struct node
{
        int value;
        struct node *leftlink,
                    *rightlink;
};
```

And now trees can easily be built as shown in Fig. 13.4.

13.4 RECURSION

This time the simplest way to write a function which can determine whether or not a specified element value exists is to write the function in such a way that it calls itself as part of its operation. This may sound a strange idea if you have not encountered it before but functions that call themselves are very useful in lots of applications in computing and are known as **recursive** functions. Remember that in C automatic local variables and parameter variables are created when a function is called and destroyed again automatically when the function terminates. This means that if a function calls

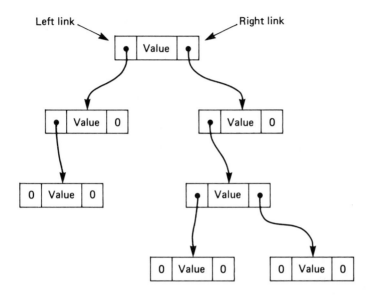

Fig. 13.4 Sample tree structure built up from nodes

itself, a new set of variables will be created with each call so that none of the values get mixed up. This is the main feature of C that makes recursion in C possible.

```
search(ptr,data)
struct node *ptr;
int data;
{
        if (ptr == NULL)
                return(0);

        if (ptr->value == data)
                return(1);

        if (search(ptr->leftlink,data))
                return(1);

        if (search(ptr->rightlink,data))
                return(1);

        return(0);
}
```

The **search** function returns an integer value of either 0 or 1. If the specified data is found it returns 1 otherwise it returns 0. Two parameters are passed into **search**. The first one is a pointer to the node structure whose value **search** will check, and the second is the data value to check for in that node. As each node has pointers to two other nodes contained within it then it is obvious that these pointers need to be followed so that their nodes can also be searched if the required data value is not found in the current node. This idea is where the recursive step comes in and it forms the basis of the solution to the problem.

The **search** function begins by checking to see if the pointer passed to it is NULL, as this indicates the end of a branch in the tree. A zero value is returned in this case to say that the required data value was not found down this branch.

Assuming now that this is not the end of a branch then the pointer is pointing to a node that needs to be checked and this is the next action. The value in this node is compared with the data parameter passed into the function. If a match is found then the value 1 is returned to the calling function to say that the **search** was successful.

If the current node does not contain the required value then the left and right subtrees need to be searched for a match. The next statement therefore calls **search** recursively with the same value of data to find but with a pointer that points to the current node's left subtree. If the required value is found down the left subtree then the recursive call to **search** will return the value 1 to say so. In this case the 1 value is returned by this function also to pass on the good news to its caller. If, however, the **search** down the left subtree returns a 0 value then the recursive **search** call is repeated down the right subtree. Again only good news is passed back to the calling function. If there is no good news then finally a 0 value is returned which says that the data value was not found in this node nor in any of the nodes below this one.

Understanding and mastering the use of recursion take a little practice, so if you are in any doubt about the operation of the **search** function then try it out on paper with a few simple examples.

13.5 STORAGE ALLOCATION

So far you have seen several functions that find their way through data structures of elements linked by pointers in various ways. However, no consideration has yet been given to where the elements are coming from in order that they may be made part of the data structures, or where the storage space for an element goes to if it should be deleted from a data structure. There are two real possibilities; the first is that an array of empty elements is declared to begin with and that these will act as a pool from which new elements can be taken and to which deleted elements can be returned.

Declaring an array of structures is straightforward enough; for example, the declaration of an array of tree nodes and a pointer to a node would be:

struct node pool[50],*ptr;

Supposing that element 26 is the next free element in the array then a pointer can be obtained to that element as expected:

```
nextfree = 26;
ptr = &pool[nextfree];
nextfree++;
```

However, one drawback with this method is that the number of elements in an array is fixed when the program is compiled and cannot be changed at run time if, for example, more elements are required than were envisaged at compile time. To overcome this problem a function call exists which can allocate a block of memory on request at run time and return a pointer to the block. The function is called **malloc**:

ptr = (struct node *) malloc(sizeof(struct node));

This looks fairly complex so I will break it down a bit. The general form of the **malloc** function call is:

malloc(size);

The parameter passed to **malloc** is the number of bytes you want to have allocated. If **malloc** can comply with your request then a pointer will be returned by **malloc** to a block of memory of the requested size (otherwise **malloc** returns a NULL pointer). The type of the returned value is a **char** pointer. If you need a pointer to some other type of object then the **char** pointer must be cast as appropriate.

With this information, the earlier example should now make sense:

sizeof(struct node)

evaluates to an integer value that is the size in bytes of the specified object. It is a good idea to use the **sizeof** operator in situations where different implementations of C could give different results. Using **malloc** on this value will make a request for an allocation of memory big enough to hold one instance of the specified object. If the memory is available a **char** pointer to the block is returned by **malloc**. This value then needs to be cast to the correct type so that it can be assigned to the variable **ptr**. The correct type in this example is a pointer to a node structure (struct node *).

When you have finished with a block of memory allocated by **malloc** it can be released back to the system with the function call:

free(ptr);

Note that the value of **ptr** must have been allocated by a previous call to **malloc**.

13.6 UNIONS

Sometimes you may want to treat a block of memory in two or more different ways. Suppose for example you have an **int** value on a machine that uses 4 byte **ints** and that for a particular application you need to split the **int** up into its four component bytes. On yet another occasion you want also to be able to extract two **short** integer values (2 bytes each) from your **int**. In both cases this can be done with a fair bit of fiddling involving bit masks and shift operations. However, the same effect can be obtained by using a **union** which will allow you to redefine the same area of memory in two or more different ways. For example:

```
union word
{
        int full;
        short half[2];
        char quarter[4];
};
```

Just as with structures, the name **word** is a tag or template name which can then be used to declare variables of this type. This allows programs like the following:

```
main()
{
        union word data;

        data.quarter[0] = 'a';
        data.quarter[1] = 'b';
        data.half[1] = -1;

        printf("%08X\n",data.full);
}
```

This example implies that the same 4-byte block of memory is being accessed in three different ways, as illustrated in Fig. 13.5.

In more practical applications, **unions** can be included as fields in structures which will allow a structure to be declared with several different versions. Each version has basically the same layout but with one or more fields that can have different types of value in different situations.

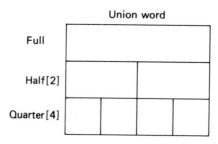

Fig. 13.5 A Union addressing the same block of memory 3 different ways

PART THREE
UNIX and C

UNIX system interface | 14

The majority of things covered in C so far will be more or less universal across all C implementations. The contents of this chapter are more specific to a UNIX or compatible environment.

14.1 LOW-LEVEL I/O

You have seen the use of **fopen, fclose, fseek, getc** and **putc** and these may have seemed pretty low-level I/O calls. However, these calls are all implemented in terms of lower-level calls still. These lower-level calls are the lowest-level access into the UNIX operating system itself and in some circumstances you will need to be able to make this level of access.

Just as at the higher level all I/O is still via files and the files still need to be associated with an I/O buffer structure. This means that an equivalent call to **fopen** is still required and, at the low level, this call becomes:

fd = open (filename, access)

using the system call **open**. The first parameter to **open** is a pointer to a '\0' terminated string (**char** array) that is the name of the file to access, and the second parameter is an **int** that specifies the type of access to allow to the file. There are several acceptable values, the three most common being:

0 read only
1 write only
2 read and write

A set of #**defines** giving these values symbolic names and listing all other possibilities is given in the file.

/usr/include/fcntl.h

The names for the three values above are:

O__RDONLY   **read only**
O__WRONLY   **write only**
O__RDWR   **read and write**

So far this is similar to **fopen**; the big difference, however, is that **open** does not return a file pointer or a pointer of any kind. In fact it returns a small integer value called a file descriptor. The file descriptor is actually the index into an array of system information that is held about each file. This is similar in principle to the data buffer that is set up when **fopen** is used on a file. Given a file pointer there is a standard #**define** contained in **stdio.h** which will act like a function call and return the value of the corresponding file descriptor:

fd = fileno(fp);

The file descriptor returned by **open** needs to be saved as it will have to be passed into any low-level I/O calls that use this file. In situations where the file does not exist a separate system call can be used to create the file for write access. Again a file descriptor is returned:

fd = creat (filename,mode)

Notice that **creat** is spelled without the 'e' on the end. The first parameter is just a pointer to the required file name string. The second parameter is a file permissions specification with which the file will be created. The permission bits are specified in the same format as the permissions in the **chmod** command.

fd = creat("testfile",0644);

would create a file called testfile with a set of permissions that would appear on an **ls −l** listing as follows:

−rw−r−−r−−

14.2 READ AND WRITE

The low-level system calls for input from and output to a file are:

numin = read(fd,buf,num);
numout = write(fd,buf,num);

The **read** call is used to take bytes from a file. The three parameters are:

fd   The file descriptor for the apropriate file

buf   A pointer to a **char** or **char** array where the bytes read will be
          stored

num   An **int** value specifying how many bytes are to be read

Obviously, the size of **buf** must be large enough to hold the number of bytes specified by **num**. The value returned by **read** is an **int** which is the number of bytes actually transferred to **buf**. Normally, this will be the same as **num** unless there are not that many bytes left in the file. A **read** request that is attempted at EOF will return the value 0.

The **write** call has the same parameters as **read** except that **num** characters are written to the file from **buf** instead of the other way. Again, the return value is the number of bytes actually transferred. But this time if the return value does not equal **num** then some sort of error has occurred. As you can see, **read** and **write** do not automatically buffer input and output characters unless you specify the buffer for yourself. This generally makes I/O using **fopen** and **putc** and **getc** more efficient at run time than the low-level I/O routines.

14.3 LOW-LEVEL RANDOM ACCESS

Obviously since random access files are available at the higher level they must be implemented in terms of low-level calls. The low-level call is very similar to its high-level counterpart:

lseek(fd,offset,base)

the only real difference is that the first parameter is a file descriptor and not a file pointer. The other two parameters are the same. **base** has values:

0 start of the file
1 current file position
2 end of the file

and **offset** is a **long** value added to the position specified by **base**.

When you have finished with a file, it is good practice to inform the system of this with a call to:

close(fd);

This is analogous to the **fclose** library call you have seen before, but uses a file descriptor instead of a file pointer.

14.4 REMOVING FILES

If you have completely finished with a file then it can be removed from the file system altogether (like using the UNIX **rm** command) by using the function:

unlink(filename);

where **filename** is a pointer to a string or **char** array holding the name of the file to delete.

14.5 I/O REDIRECTION

Up to now you have only considered I/O redirection as though it was just a facility provided by the **shell**. Do not forget though that the **shell** itself is only a C program like any other, and anything it can do for you, you can do for yourself.

Programs that are intended to be used with I/O redirection are generally written using the function calls **getchar**, **putchar**, **printf** and **scanf**. All these calls make use of the **stdin** and **stdout** file pointers. The corresponding file descriptors are:

0 stdin
1 stdout
2 stderr

These are defined in **stdio.h** and will always have these values.

I/O redirection involves changing the files associated with file descriptors 0 and 1 (usually) for some other files so that calls to **getchar**, **putchar**, etc. while still using the same file pointers and descriptors will actually be accessing different files. You remember I said that the information accessible via the file descriptors is stored in an array, and that the file descriptor itself is just an index into the appropriate array element. Well, when a file descriptor is allocated on an **open** or **creat** system call, the system automatically searches this array from element 0 looking for a free element to use for the file. This means that the system will always find the lowest numbered file descriptor that is available and allocate it to the file being opened.

This fact can be used to perform all the UNIX I/O redirection facilities given the existence of an extra system function called **dup**:

fd2 = dup(fd1);

What **dup** does is to make a duplicate copy of a file descriptor so that two different file descriptors both access the same file. The parameter passed into **dup** is the file descriptor to be duplicated and the return value is the copy file descriptor that results. Like **open** and **creat**, **dup** will take the lowest numbered file descriptor that is available when it allocates the new one. With this information, redirecting the standard output say to the file 'newout' is quite straightforward:

```
fd = dup (1);              /* save current fd[1] */
close (1);                 /* close, stdout */
creat ("newout",0600);     /*'newout' uses fd[1] */

───────────              /* standard output now */
───────────              /* goes to file 'newout' */

close (1);                 /* Restore fd[1] to */
dup (fd);                  /* original destination */
close (fd);                /* and tidy up */
```

In this example, the standard output is redirected in such a way that it can be restored to its previous destination afterwards. This is done by duplicating the standard output file descriptor into variable **fd** before closing file descriptor 1 and creating the file **newout** over the top. When you have finished sending standard output to **newout** the file can be closed and the original destination restored by duplicating the saved value of **fd** back into the newly released file descriptor 1. All that has to be done to finish off is just to close the temporary file descriptor stored in **fd**.

14.6. PIPES

As well as redirecting input and output to files they can also be redirected into and out of a pipe. You remember that the **shell** can set up a pipe between two programs so that the output of one can be channelled straight into the input of another:

$ **who** | **wc** **−1**

This example sends the output from **who** into the **wc** program which counts the number of lines (**−1**) in its input. Taken as a single command this line will tell you how many users are currently logged on to the system.

The pipe itself is actually a 'fifo' buffer which means that the first item of data written into it will be the first item to be read when it emerges at the other end ('fifo' means 'first in first out'). This means that with a pipe there are two access points, one that you write to and one that you read from. The ends of the pipe are thus allocated two file descriptors when the pipe is opened, one for each end.

A pipe is created and opened with the system call:

pipe(fd);

where **fd** is declared to be a two-element **int** array into which the two file descriptors will be copied:

int fd[2];

The file descriptor returned in **fd[0]** is the one for the **read** end of the pipe and **fd[1]** is the file descriptor for the **write** end. The **pipe** function itself does return a value; this is 0 if the call is successful and −1 otherwise.

You remember in Chapter 3 that I said that the **shell** executes a **fork** system call when it wants to run another program and that this call creates a complete copy of the calling program. The UNIX system then arranges to run both the calling program (the parent) and the duplicate copy (the child) at the same time. So exact is the copy made of the parent process, that even file descriptors that have been allocated when the copy takes place will be available to the child process as well.

This means that if the parent process creates a pipe and then performs a **fork** system call, the child will also have access to the pipe as well. All that now needs to be done is for the parent to write to the pipe or redirect its standard output to the **fd[1]** file descriptor and for the child to read from the pipe or redirect its standard input to the **fd[0]** file descriptor and the two processes, parent and child, are in communication with each other. The **fork** system call will be covered later in the chapter but once a pipe has been opened and the **fork** call made, connecting the two processes together is easy. In the parent it becomes:

```
fd = dup (1);            /* redirect standard output */
close (1);               /* to the pipe */
dup (fd[1]);
close (fd[1]);
                         /* communicate here */

close (1);               /* restore standard output */
dup (fd);                /* back to normal */
close (fd);
```

and in the child process the connection can be completed with:

```
fd = dup (0);            /* redirect standard input */
close (0);               /* from the pipe */
dup (fd[0]);
close (fd[0]);

                         /* communicate here */

close (0);               /* restore standard input */
dup (fd);                /* back to normal */
close (fd);
```

This type of procedure allows a pipe to be set up between any two processes as long as they have common ancestors to set up the pipes for them in the first place. For any two arbitrary processes to communicate with each other requires the use of a named pipe.

14.7. NAMED PIPES

A named pipe is a special sort of file which has 'fifo' properties so that one process can write to the pipe and another can read from it. The system ensures that data written to the pipe is properly queued and that data is removed from the pipe as it is read.

A special system call has to be used to create the named pipe in the first place, but once created it can be opened for **read** and **write** operations just like an ordinary file. The special call is **mknod**:

mknod (filename,filetype);

The first parameter is a pointer to the file name as usual. The second parameter consists of a six-digit number; the first three digits are 010 and the last three digits are the permission bits for **read/write** access to the pipe's owner, group and others (see the UNIX **chmod** command for a complete description of the permission bits). For example:

mknod ("pipe",010666);

would create a 'fifo' file called pipe that would give the following listing to the **ls** command:

```
$ ls —l pipe
prw—rw—rw— 1 pc              pc               0 Apr 8 16:08 pipe
```

Notice that the first data bit in field 1 contains a new character (p) to indicate that this file is a pipe. Also notice that on creation, field 5 of this listing shows the file to be empty (0).

Two unrelated programs can now **open** this pipe, one for **read** access and one for **write** access, and communicate with each other as though this was a normal pipe. Using the file descriptors returned when named pipes are opened they can also be used for redirected standard I/O as well. Here is an example of the sending and redirecting its standard output to a named pipe:

```
fd = open ("pipe",O__WRONLY);
fdtmp = dup (1);
close (1);
dup (fd);
```

After communication has finished the standard output can be restored to normal using the saved file descriptor in **fdtmp**.

14.8 EXECUTING COMMANDS

Sometimes it may happen that you wish to run one of the standard UNIX commands or one of your own commands from within your program. The simplest way to do this is by using one of the functions built into the standard C library. The function is:

system (command);

where the **command** parameter is a pointer to a string containing the name of the command to execute plus any parameters to pass to that command. For example:

system ("ls −l");

After the command specified in the **system** call has executed, control is returned to your program which continues to run.

The underlying system calls that control process execution are quite simple and indeed you have met them briefly already in Chapter 3. The main call that allows new processes to be created is called **fork**:

pid = fork ( );

Notice that the call has no parameters passed to it. When executed, the **fork** call duplicates your currently running process exactly so that two identical copies of your program exist. After duplication both copies of your program continue to run, one called the parent and the other called the child. The only difference between the two processes is the value returned to them by the **fork** call. In the case of the child process, its version of the **fork** call returns the value 0. In the case of the parent the value returned is non-zero, in fact it is the process identity number of the child process. This is the same process ID number that is returned by the standard UNIX **ps** command. Because **fork** returns a different value to the two processes each of them can tell which one of the two it is, and so perform actions accordingly:

---

if ((pid = fork ( )) ! = 0)

{

    /* perform parent actions */

}
else
{

    /* perform child actions */

}

In the case of the **shell**, after it has performed the **fork** call the child process needs to execute your specified command. What needs to happen then is that the current child process, which in the case of the **shell** is just a copy of the **shell**, needs to be replaced by a copy of the program that you want to execute.

This action is performed by the **exec** system call. In fact there are several closely related versions of **exec** each offering slightly different facilities. Probably the most useful version is called **execlp**.

The general format of the **execlp** call is:

execlp (command,paramlist . . .);

The first parameter is a pointer to the file name of the command that is to be executed. Within that command there will be a function **main** (assuming it is written in C) and you remember that the entire contents of the command line is passed to **main** as a pointer to an array of pointers. Each of the pointers in the array points to one of the words on the command line. The name of the pointer is **argv** by convention. The **execlp** second and subsequent parameters are the individual strings that will be accessible to **argv** in the new command.

execlp ("ls","ls","−l",NULL);

This **execlp** call will therefore execute the **ls** command (first parameter) and pass the strings:

"ls"   **as argv[0]**
"−l"   **as argv[1]**
" "   **as argv[2]**

Notice that the list of parameters to **execlp** is terminated by a NULL pointer; this is so that the number of parameters in **argv** can be counted and **argv** set up accordingly.

Sometimes the number of parameters following the initial command name will not be known. For example, the **shell** does not know in advance what commands you are likely to enter at the keyboard nor how many parameters you will type after the command. In cases like this all you need to do is to build up a pointer array like **argv** for yourself and then call a version of **exec** with just two parameters. The first parameter is again a pointer to the file name to execute but this time the second parameter is a pointer to the array of pointers you have built up. A call to this version of **exec** appears as:

execvp (filename,paramptr);

Incidentally, both **execlp** and **execvp** will use the value of the environment variable **$PATH**, just like the **shell**, to sort out which directories to search for the specified 'filename'.

Once an **exec** call has been successfully performed there is no attempt made to return to the process that was running before the call. There is no point, as the old process has been overlaid by the new one in all of the internal tables of UNIX and so there is nothing left to return to. This means that at the end of execution the child process just terminates.

The parent process after execution of **fork** has two choices: it can either get on and do something else or it can opt to wait for its child to terminate. The latter choice is made with the **wait** system call:

pid = wait (&status);

Executing **wait** puts a parent process to sleep until any of its child processes terminates at which time the parent will be reawakened. The return value from **wait** is the process ID number of the particular child that terminated. The parent can then compare the value with the pid returned by the **fork** call when the child was created to see which child has terminated. The paramater passed to **wait** is a pointer to an **int** variable which can be used by the child to inform the parent of its termination status.

If the child wishes to send an exit status value back to the parent when it terminates it can do so with the system call **exit**;

exit (status);

By convention if a child terminates normally with no error conditions pending it will return a zero status value. Other status values can be used to convey any desired meaning and are not reserved in any way. If no specific status value is returned by a child then some indeterminate value will be returned. Therefore it is always best to use **exit** at the end of a program, even if the status value you return is just fixed at zero.

14.9 SIGNALS

In UNIX information about certain events can be sent to a process by means of a signal. One example of a signalled event is an interrupt from the keyboard. Another possibility is a request to send a signal by another program. In all cases the default action taken when a process is signalled is to terminate the receiving process. With the exception of one special signal, it is possible for the process to opt to change this default action. Either specified signals can be ignored or they can cause a call to a predefined function within the receiving program whose action will presumably deal with the signal.

The most useful and common signals are:

SIGINT   This is the interrupt signal from the terminal keyboard (usually the DEL key)

SIGQUIT   The quit signal is also generated from the keyboard, but as well as terminating the process it also causes a dump of all its memory map into a file called **core** which can later be read and analysed. This signal is usually generated by typing ctrl–\ at the terminal

SIGKILL   This is the special signal that cannot be ignored or trapped; it is a sure way to kill a process

SIGALRM   This is the signal that is sent to a process as an alarm indication after a previously set time has elapsed

SIGTERM   This signal is usually used as the software termination signal. If it is trapped then the process usually uses this signal to perform some clean-up operations before terminating voluntarily in a tidy state

SIGUSR1
SIGUSR2   These are used for user-defined actions

In order to change the action of a signal from the default which will terminate the process, you use the system call **signal**:

signal (name,action);

The first parameter to **signal** is the name of the signal whose action you wish to modify. The second parameter is the name of a function that will be executed if the signal should occur. There are also two special values for the second parameter that can be used:

SIG__DFL Restores the signal's default action

SIG__IGN Ignores the signal altogether

The definitions for these names and the names of the signals themselves appear in the file **<signal.h>** which should be #included at the start of your program if you need to use signals.

The value returned by **signal** is the current value of its second parameter so that the value can be restored later if required.

Whenever a signal is trapped to one of your own functions and that signal occurs then the signal routine will automatically revert to SIG__DFL so that inside your signal trap function you will need to re-enable the signal trap. For example to catch SIGTERM:

```
#include <signal.h>

int sigflag = 0;

trapper()
{
        signal(SIGTERM,trapper);        /* re-arm signal */
        sigflag++;                      /* record the event */
}


main()
{
        signal(SIGTERM,trapper);        /* initial setup */

        /* Rest of main program */
        /* goes in here */
}
```

14.10 SENDING SIGNALS

A signal of any type can be sent by one process to another using the system call **kill**. The general form of a **kill** call is:

kill (pid,signame);

This call sends the signal whose name is given as the second parameter to the process having the specified process ID in the first parameter. If the signal cannot be sent then **kill** returns the value −1. If a process ID of 0 (otherwise an unused pid) is used then all processes belonging to the current user will be sent the signal **signame**.

C debugging and program maintenance | 15

By now you have seen examples showing most of what C has to offer. There are, however, several details which though not strictly part of C need to be covered in order to help you get your programs working and to keep them going through any later modifications.

In fact there are one or two pitfalls in C which can easily trip the unwary and which I shall mention so that you may have a chance to recognize the symptoms in your own programs.

15.1 PITFALLS IN C

The C compiler produces very compact and efficient object code as its output. If this were not the case it would be unsuitable as a system programming language for its code would be too large and slow for applications like writing UNIX. In order to make the compiler so efficient certain shortcuts have had to be taken in its construction. This means that there are certain aspects of the language that you as a programmer have to take responsibility for, which the compiler would take care of for you in other languages.

For instance, the standard C compiler does not check that the numbers or types of parameters that you pass into a function match those specified in the actual function declaration. In other words the compiler would not complain if you did something like the following:

```
main()
{
        int a = 1, b = 2;
        char c = 'a';

        test(a,b,c);
        test();
}


test(x,y)
float x;
char *y;
{
        /* Body of function test */
}
```

Here you can see two calls of the function **test** from within **main**. The first call passes three parameters to **test**, two **ints** and a **char**. The second call to test passes no parameters at all. To complicate things still further the function **test** itself is declared to expect two parameters, a **float** and a **char** pointer!

Amid all this confusion the compiler will sail on blindly and uncomplaining. When it compiles **main** it will generate code to pass only the parameters given in the function calls without making any check of the function requirements. And when it compiles **test** it will generate code to take the parameter values that have been declared from where they are expected to be without any check that they are actually there.

This can lead to all sorts of complications. No one is suggesting that you will make errors on the scale of the previous example but in a long program for instance it is easy to pass a pair of parameters reversed and not notice. Even if the reversed parameters are of different types the compiler will not spot the error, where in other languages the compiler would certainly not let the error pass. This policy for no parameter checking on function calls is not all bad news. It does allow the existence of functions like **printf** and **scanf** and system calls like **execlp** where the numbers and types of parameters cannot be specified because they can change from call to call.

15.2 C EXPRESSION PROBLEMS

As you have seen, one of the great advantages in C is that C treats most things as expressions that carry values. This allows all sorts of optimizations that are not permitted in other languages but which add to the efficiency and compactness of compiled C code.

Several examples that should appear familiar to you are:

while (*str1++ = *str2++);

which conventionally would be something like:

```
*str1 = *str2
while (*str1 != '\0')
{
     str1 = str1 + 1;
     str2 = str2 + 1;
     *str1 = *str2;
}
```

Notice in the compact version that the pointers **str1** and **str2** are referenced twice altogether whereas in the version made to resemble the actions that would be required in a more conventional language they are referenced nine times. In terms of execution times this is a very significant difference especially as a loop is involved which will greatly magnify the difference. Another example might be:

printf ("%d %d\n", x = 5, z = (y < 0) ? −1 : 1);

Again in a conventional language this would end up something like:

```
x = 5;
if (y < 0)
     z = (−1);
else
     z = 1;

printf ("%d %d\n", x, z);
```

However, everything has its price and this economy of code is no exception. When there are very few restrictions on how an expression is put together then it is only too easy to write something that looks like the intended expression but which acts in a totally different way. For example:

```
while (x = 3)
{
     /* actions in here */
}
```

Here the intention is that some sequence of actions will take place repeatedly, until the value of **x** is no longer equal to 3.

However, because of the use of a similar but incorrect operator, the construct will perform the controlled actions for ever. This program fragment should have been:

```
while (x == 3)
{
    /* actions in here */
}
```

using the equality comparison operator (==) and not the assignment operator (=) as before. As the assignment operator like all the others in C returns a value, the C compiler will just generate code to evaluate the expression and use its value in the conditional test. You might imagine that there are certain constructs such as this that the C compiler could spot and report as errors. However, there are circumstances when the expression you are trying to trap may be just the one you need. And besides it would make learning C very difficult if there was a set of simple rules for building any expressions you liked, and then a set of exceptions to cover situations where particular types of expression might not be used.

The practical upshot of all these examples is that simple typing errors which would often be detected in other languages at compile time will frequently cause no errors for the C compiler and will therefore not come to light and cause problems until run time. Unfortunately at run time it will be difficult to sort out whether the symptoms of a problem you observe are caused by a simple typing error or basic logic error in the program. Just these problems alone make C generally more difficult to debug than otherwise similar languages.

15.3 POINTER PROBLEMS

Unfortunately what you have seen so far is just the simple end of the difficulty. The use of pointers opens up a whole new dimension of possibilities for problems — a real Pandora's box! Really to appreciate the difficulty you will need a little bit of information about the stack arrangement that the C compiler uses for a function call. Consider the following code fragment:

```
test1 ()
{
    char text[10];
    test2 (text);
}
test2 (ptr)
char *ptr;
{
    /* The array text[] can be */
    /* accessed here via ptr */
}
```

What you see here are two simple functions. The first declares a ten-element **char** array and then passes a pointer to the start of this array as a parameter to the second function. As you have already seen, by using suitable pointer arithmetic the pointer variable **ptr** in **test2** can be used to access all the elements in the **text** array in **test1**. In 'C' local variable contents, parameter values in function calls and function call return addresses are all stored on the machine stack at run time. Suppose the pointer in **test2** were to be incremented or decremented outside the limits of the **text** array in **test1**. What would happen then? Well, nothing really, unless the pointer was used for writing a value into a location outside the array. Remember that as well as storing this array on the stack all the other local variables are also stored there. This immediately allows a runaway pointer to access other variables within the function it should point to. But worse than that it also allows access to the local variables in any of the functions that are on the execution path to the current function as the local variables for all of them are on the stack. The effect of this sort of error is that a local variable will unpredictably change its value within a function. And do not forget that the change could have been made by any function that the current function calls, either directly or indirectly.

As I have already said, local variable values are not the only thing stored on the stack. The value of parameters passed to functions are stored there also and these are equally vulnerable to pointer problems and with similar results. At least these problems only change the values of a variable.

When one function calls another an address is stored on the stack to tell the machine where to return to in the calling function when the called function is finished. If you have had any dealings with machine code then you will be familiar with this idea. Just by chance, what is there to stop a runaway pointer from overwriting a return address? Sadly the answer is nothing! And bugs of this kind can really cause some headaches, for instead of returning to the calling function at the proper place the return can be made to anywhere. It may only be a few bytes away from the proper place or a long way away. One thing is for sure — the result is totally unpredictable.

```
bad( );
printf ("I got here");
next( );
/* rest of code */
```

Suppose for example that within the function **bad** the return address to this block of code is being incremented in error by a number of bytes. Normally the return address from **bad** will cause the **printf** statement to execute. It is possible, however, that the new return address could cause the **printf** statement to be skipped altogether, continuing instead with the call to **next**.

If you ran this program I am sure you would be quite surprised to discover that function **bad** seems to run OK and that function **next** also runs OK, but that the **printf** between them does not do anything. Where would you look for that error? And do not forget that this is quite a well-behaved example; the return address could be changed to anything. To make matters worse, this is not the only scenario that can result in that **printf** statement failing to perform its task. Consider this:

```
#include <stdio.h>

char pass[] = "XXXXXXX";

main()
{
        int c,i;

        for (i = 0; (c = getchar()) != '\n' && i < 8; i++)
                pass[i] = c;

        pass[i] = '\0';

        printf("The password is");
        printf(" %s\n",pass);
}
```

Here an external **char** array eight elements long is declared called **pass**. This will be used to hold a password entered at the keyboard. The keyboard characters are taken in a **for** loop one at a time with a **getchar** call. While a count (**i**) of the number of characters read is less than eight and the character read is not a newline, then the characters are stored in consecutive elements of the **pass** array. When the password has been entered and the **for** loop has terminated then a **0** is stored at the end of the password to make it into a C string. Finally a message is printed ("The password is") followed by the password that was entered. Simple!

OK. Run the program and enter the password:

UNIXANDC

all as one word, followed by pressing return and you will probably find that the message:

The password is

does not get printed while the password itself does. In other words, the first **printf** line fails to function but the second one works just fine. Now what is the problem?

This one has to do with the layout of static and external storage space. You remember that string constants are stored in static memory and then generate a pointer to the start of the string. In this program there are three string constants. They are:

"XXXXXXX"
"The password is"
"%s\n"

and they would normally be stored in memory one after the other, separated by the \0 characters that are added as string terminators by C. In addition, three pointer constants would be set up to point to the start of each of the strings. These pointer values will be used wherever the strings appeared in the program. Notice that the first string in the example program is eight elements long (seven for characters and \0) and is used to initialize the **char** array called **pass**. All that happens on initialization is that **pass** is given the value of the pointer that points to the initialization string (**XXXXXXX**). Storing any characters in the **pass** array will just overwrite the appropriate characters in this string.

When you type in your password then, it is stored in static memory. Now, remember that pointers can point anywhere unchecked, and that pointers and arrays are two sides of the same coin. You should not then be surprised to discover that the C compiler at compile time and at run time does not check that array subscripts stay within the bounds declared for an array.

If in the current example an array subscript outside the range 0–7 were to be used in the **pass** array then it would be possible to overwrite other areas of static memory (such as those holding the other string constant values).

If you look closely at the program you will find when an eight-character password is typed that all eight characters will be entered into **pass[0]**to **pass[7]** and then a \0 will be placed as a terminator into the non-existent **pass[8]**.

The location of **pass[8]** is in fact the first character of the string:

The password is

This means that anything pointing to the string (like the first **printf** line) will actually be pointing directly at a string terminator, so the first **printf** will not print very much. The second **printf** works fine, however, as both of the strings it accesses are intact. The simplest solution to the problem is to add an extra **X** to the **pass** initialization string.

Most programmers who have used standard debugging techniques with normal languages find that their expectations about how the system should operate are so automatic and deep-seated that they tend to invent the most unlikely explanations to account for their problems. Something like, 'there must be a bug in the compiler' is commonly reported to me by perplexed students.

15.4 WRITING MAINTAINABLE C

Sadly there is no magic wand that can be waved that helps to take away these problems in all situations or on all machines. Some machine-dependent routines are possible to help you track back in the stack at various places in the program to make sure that it holds reasonable values. But there are too many variations possible for me to be able to give listings.

The best alternative then is to prevent the problems from occurring in the first place. In C it is most certainly true that prevention is better than cure, and probably a lot easier.

Having said earlier that the C compiler does not check for function call parameter numbers and types and other dubious though legal expressions, there is a program that does — it is called **lint**.

The **lint** program should be used instead of **cc**. It is very thorough and will probably produce a lot of output most of which you will be able to ignore. However, just occasionally it will turn up something unexpected that needs attention. The output from the **lint** program is different on different machines and it is a good idea to get used to the version you have available to you by using it to start with on known good programs to see the sorts of things that it will warn you about.

15.5 MODULARITY

After that you have to write your programs in a way that makes testing and modification as easy and trouble-free as possible. One idea that can be implemented very easily in C is modularity.

What this means is that you break the solution to a programming problem down into smaller and more manageable units, each of which is functionally independent of the others. In C each of the modules can correspond with a function. Any particular module should have a well-defined input specification, a well-defined output specification and a well-defined job to do. The modules themselves are just black boxes in that it does not matter to the rest of a program how a particular module performs its task as long as it does perform it.

As a simple example consider a program to take a set of numbers from standard input, sort them into ascending order and print them out to the standard output.

Most sort algorithms work well on an array structure so this suggests a three-module solution to the problem. The first module will read a set of values until EOF, say, into an array of **int**. The second module will sort the array into order and put the result back into the same array. The third module will then take the contents of the array and send the values to the standard output.

With modular programs one of the big advantages is that different modules can be written by different programmers so that a program can be a team effort. In this case it is best if a particular programmer just needs to know what input will be presented to the module, what output will be expected from the module and the job the module will be expected to perform. It is a good idea to use as few global variables in these situations as possible so that there can be no conflict in names or format of data. In fact the only global variable in the example problem would probably be the array to hold the values.

This allows a **main** program to be written as follows:

```c
#include <stdio.h>
#include "defs.h"

int values[MAXARRAY];

main()
{
        input();
        sort();
        output();
}
```

This is a top-down design and programming method and it is a good idea to test each function properly as soon as it is written. In this case the function is very trivial and I would be prepared to accept that it will work. However, you should not allow functions much more complex than this to go untested; a lot of C bugs are subtle and need to be caught early.

This just leaves the three module functions to write. The **input** function will take **int** values from the standard input device and store them in the **values** array. When the module is written a simple test harness can be constructed to see that it works. This will consist of calling the function and then printing the **values** array contents when the function has finished to check visually that all is as it should be.

In the same way, **sort** and **output** modules can be written and tested. Finally all the bits can be brought together and tested as a whole.

This technique has allowed a program to be split into manageable and independent pieces. Each of the pieces can be given to different programmers to write if the program is to be a team effort. If the program is for one programmer to write, then splitting the program into independent modules means that the programmer can concentrate on one small part of the program at a time without worrying about this module's interactions with the rest of the project. Each of the modules can be independently tested. Once you have a set of useful modules (such as the **sort** module for example) they can be reused on other projects, just like the standard C library. And the biggest bonus of all is that modularity allows easier maintenance and modification.

Suppose that to get the project working quickly you had written a rather slow but simple **sort** routine. If its speed proves to be a problem you can always take the original input and output specifications for the module and write a new **sort** routine using a better or faster algorithm. When the new module is written and tested it can just be slotted into the existing system without any changes to the rest of the modules. This is because the rest of the system treats the **sort** module as a black box anyway. Other modules do not know when it changes as long as the input and output specifications remain the same.

Another idea that makes sense as far as modularity is concerned is to keep sets of related modules in separate files so that, for example, in an interpreter program one file may contain all the modules and functions related to expression evaluation while another file contains the modules for executing program statements and so on.

15.5 MAKE

When a program is split up over several files, the C compiler can arrange to compile them all separately and then link the resulting files together at the end. If, for example, you have a program consisting of the three files called:

prog1.c   **prog2.c**   **prog3.c**

then they can all be compiled and combined together with the command:

$ **cc prog1.c   prog2.c   prog3.c   −o program**

As each of the individual C files is compiled an object file will be produced with the same name but with the '**.c**' replaced with a '**.o**', i.e. files called:

prog1.o   **prog2.o**   **prog3.o**

will be produced. When all three files have been compiled the three '**.o**' files will be combined into one executable program called **program** as specified on the command line.

As your programs get larger and larger and hence take up more and more source files the command that needs to be typed and the time taken to compile all the files gets longer and longer. In fact when you change the contents of a file there is not really much point in compiling all the other files because they have not changed. All you need to do is to specify the **.o** file names on the command line instead of the **.c** names and the existing unchanged object files will be linked in with the new object file from the source file that needed compiling. For example, if file **prog2.c** is modified then only that file needs to be compiled. The resulting new **.o** file **prog2.o** can then be linked in with the other existing **.o** files using the command:

$ **cc prog1.o   prog2.c   prog3.o   −o program**

Again this becomes very tedious when lots of files are involved even if it does not take so long to compile any more.

To finish off, I shall describe the simple use of a UNIX utility program that can automate the whole process. This utility is called **make**.

In essence what **make** does is to take a look at any files you tell it to and see if they have been modified since the last time **make** looked. If the files have changed then **make** will execute any commands you specify.

Obviously in the case of C programs you get **make** to look at all your source files and if any of them have changed you just tell **make** to recompile your program. With a little care you can get **make** only to recompile the source files that have been changed. A **make** command file for the three-file C program example could be:

```
program:        prog1.o prog2.o prog3.o
                cc prog1.o prog2.o prog3.o -o program

prog1.o:        prog1.c
                cc -c prog1.c

prog2.o:        prog2.c
                cc -c prog2.c

prog3.o:        prog3.c
                cc -c prog3.c
```

The default command file name for **make** is called **makefile**. So a text file with this name should be created and the lines above entered into it. Working down the file from the top it says that **program** depends on the files **prog1.o**, **prog2.o** and **prog3.o** and that if any of those files has changed since the last time **make** looked then the command line below should be executed. This command will just link the three object files back together again and call the result **program**. The next line says that the file **prog1.o** depends on **prog1.c** and that if this file has changed, the command:

$ **cc** −c **prog1.c**

should be executed. The −**c** parameter to **cc** just tells it to stop the compilation process at the **.o** file stage so this command just regenerates **prog1.o** from **prog1.c** if **prog1.c** changed since **make** was last run.

The rest of the file performs the same way on **prog2.c** and **prog3.c**.

All you need to do to make sure that the whole suite of programs (however large) is all up to date is just to type:

$ **make**

and any source files that need to be recompiled will be so, then all the object files will be relinked into a single executable program.

16	# C in action

You have now covered the basics of programming in a UNIX environment using both shell scripts and C. So far only relatively simple example programs have been presented to illustrate the concepts you have seen. To finish off I shall present you with a somewhat larger example which will fall into two parts. The first part will use a C program for its solution and the second part will use a shell script. The problem itself will involve the construction of a simple compiler which will operate on a small subset of the programming language BASIC and will generate executable assembly language as its output.

First, I should point out that it is not my intention to delve into the depths of commercial compiler construction techniques. All that you will see are a few simple ideas, many of which you may already be familiar with.

The majority of the work of a real compiler consists of tracking down and reporting errors in your source code. Far more compilation runs are performed that produce error reports than produce runable code. This is obvious because as soon as you get a program that works you do not compile it again. This means that you only tend to compile a fully working program once, whereas it may have been compiled many times to get it to its working state. Some compiler error detection and recovery techniques are very complex and it is in the area of error detection where most of the simplifications in the example compiler have been made. The other main simplification is in the source language itself, which is only a very small subset of BASIC.

16.1 THE TINY BASIC SOURCE LANGUAGE

A TINY BASIC program will consist of a set of lines of code. Each line consists of two parts, the first part is a line number and the second part is a statement that details the action to be performed by the line. Line numbers in BASIC have two functions. They are used to specify the execution sequence of lines in ascending line number order and they are also used as labels to be the targets of conditional and unconditional jump statements. The statements themselves are made up of numbers, variables, expressions and keywords as follows.

16.1.1 Numbers

All numbers in TINY BASIC are signed integers, which will have a 16-bit or 32-bit range depending on your C compiler and the word size of the target assembly language and processor.

16.1.2 Variables

TINY BASIC supports integer variables which have names consisting entirely of a list of lower-case letters. Examples of valid and invalid variable names are:

Valid	Invalid
a	a1
var	var_a
fred	Fred

The maximum length of a variable name will depend on the maximum allowable length of a label to your assembler but is usually at least six to eight characters.

16.1.3 Operators

=	equal
< >	not equal
< =	less than or equal
> =	greater than or equal
<	less than
>	greater than
+	add
−	subtract (binary)
*	multiply
/	divide
−	minus (unary)

Add, subtract, multiply, divide and minus operators all give integer results with the same numeric range as numbers. The other (comparison) operators all result in a value non-zero (1) if the comparison is true and 0 if it is false. Notice in BASIC that '=' is used where '==' is used in C and that '< >' is used instead of '!='. Other BASIC operators are the same as their 'C' equivalents.

16.1.4 Expressions

Expressions are formed in BASIC from numbers and variables with operators between them. A minus (−) sign can be used before any operand in an expression to negate the value of that operand before it is used in the rest of the expression. The operator precedence is: minus, then multiply and divide, then add and subtract, then finally the comparisons. Operators of equal precedence are evaluated left to right as normal. Brackets can be used to alter the order of evaluation. A few examples are:

$(x>y)*123+(x=y)*456+(x<y)*789$

Here is the equivalent of a conditional expression. If x is greater than y then the expression evaluates to 123. If x equals y then the result is 456, and if x is less than y a value of 789 is returned.

$(u=1)*(u<2) + (u<99)*(u>3)$

Here is the equivalent of a logical expression with '*' performing the logical AND function and '+' performing the logical OR function. Logical AND has higher precedence than logical OR. Remember here that as in C any non-zero value represents TRUE and a zero value represents FALSE.

16.1.5 Keywords

In TINY BASIC there are only five different statement keywords but they are sufficient to express most programming ideas.

The first statement keyword is **LET**. This is the assignment statement in BASIC where the value of an expression is assigned to a variable. For example:

```
let x=6
let y=(x+3)*w
let total=price+tax
```

In common with most versions of BASIC, TINY BASIC treats the **LET** keyword as optional, so that the following assignments are equally valid:

```
y=9
w=a+j*b
```

Notice that assignment in BASIC uses the same operator (=) as comparison for equality. This means that:

```
a=b=5
```

assigns the value 0 or 1 (FALSE or TRUE) to the variable a. This is because the first (=) is treated as an assignment operator while the second (=) is treated as a test for the equality of b and 5.

The second statement keyword implemented in TINY BASIC is **IF/ THEN**. The TINY BASIC **IF/THEN** statement allows conditional branching to a specified line number depending on the value (TRUE/FALSE) of a conditional expression. For example:

if x=6 then 20

This says that if the variable x has the value 6 (i.e. the expression x=6 yields a non-zero value) then a jump should be made to the program line with the line number 20. If the conditional expression has a 0 (FALSE) value then execution of the program continues on the line following the **IF** statement.

The third keyword is **PRINT**. This keyword is followed by any numeric expression, the value of which should be output to the user's terminal:

print (x+7)/y

The fourth keyword is **GOTO**. This statement keyword provides an unconditional branch to a specified line number:

goto 50

The **GOTO** statement can be used in conjunction with the **IF** statement to implement the equivalent of a while loop as you will see.

The final statement keyword is **STOP**. This is just used to terminate execution of the BASIC program and return control back to the machine monitor or operating system.

A typical program using these facilities would look like the following:

```
10 a = 10
20 let b = 20
30 c = 30
40 if a*b >= 12*c then 80
50 print -a-5
60 a = a+1
70 goto 40
80 print a*a
90 stop
```

Specifying TINY BASIC in this way has probably given you a feel for the language and how its constructs go together. However, before a program can be written to translate a TINY BASIC source program into something else a much more formal definition of the TINY BASIC syntax needs to be prepared. This needs to be done so that there is no ambiguity in the language definition.

16.2 BACKUS-NAUR FORM (BNF)

The method I shall use to specify the syntax of TINY BASIC is called BNF. This method just declares a set of symbols that make up the language and then a set of rules showing what each of the symbols consists of and how the symbols can be combined. Each of the BNF rules has the form:

< defined item > ::= 'definition'

The symbol $::=$ is a BNF symbol which means 'is defined as'. Wherever a word or phrase in a 'definition' is enclosed in angle brackets $<>$ that word or phrase is itself the $<$defined item$>$ in another rule. Any items enclosed in square brackets [] are optional. Three dots . . . following an item mean that the item may be repeated zero or more times. Items on separate lines within a 'definition' or items separated by the | symbol are choices from which one must be selected. For example:

$<$program$>$ $::=$ $<$line$>$ [$<$line$>$] . . .

This says that $<$**program**$>$ is defined as a $<$**line**$>$ followed optionally and repeatedly by any number of other $<$**line**$>$s. The fact that $<$**line**$>$ is enclosed in angle brackets shows that there will be another definition to specify what the internal structure of a $<$line$>$ can be.

$<$digit$>$ $::=$ 0|1|2|3|4|5|6|7|8|9

This rule says that $<$**digit**$>$ can be any **one** of the given symbols 0–9. The fact that these symbols do not appear in angle brackets means that they are not further defined and should therefore just be typed into programs as shown.

The full BNF specification for TINY BASIC is given below. The rules are in alphabetical order of defined item. You should start with the rule for $<$**program**$>$:

```
     <addop>    ::=   + | -

     <digit>    ::=   0|1|2|3|4|5|6|7|8|9

      <expr>    ::=   <exp1> [<relop> <exp1>]...

      <exp1>    ::=   <exp2> [<addop> <exp2>]...

      <exp2>    ::=   <exp3> [<multop> <exp3>]...

      <exp3>    ::=   [-] ( <expr> )
                      [-] <number>
                      [-] <variable>

 <gotophrase>   ::=   goto <linenum>

   <ifphrase>   ::=   if <expr> then <linenum>

    <letter>    ::=   a|b|c|d|e|f|g|h|i|j|k|l|m
                      n|o|p|q|r|s|t|u|v|w|x|y|z

  <letphrase>   ::=   [let] <variable> = <expr>

      <line>    ::=   <linenum> <statement>

   <linenum>    ::=   <number>

    <multop>    ::=   * | /

    <number>    ::=   <digit> [<digit>]...
```

```
<printphrase>  ::=  print <expr>

   <program>  ::=  <line> [<line>]...

     <relop>  ::=  = | <> | <= | >= | < | >

 <statement>  ::=  <gotophrase>
                   <ifphrase>
                   <letphrase>
                   <printphrase>
                   <stopphrase>

<stopphrase>  ::=  stop

  <variable>  ::=  <letter> [<letter>]...
```

All the rules in this specification are fairly straightforward with the possible exception of the syntax for an expression. Notice that this section is not just a single rule but a set of four:

```
<expr>  ::=  <exp1> [<relop> <exp1>]...

<exp1>  ::=  <exp2> [<addop> <exp2>]...

<exp2>  ::=  <exp3> [<multop> <exp3>]...

<exp3>  ::=  [-] ( <expr> )
             [-] <number>
             [-] <variable>
```

Expressions are arranged in this way in order to get the operator precedence right. Notice also that the definition for **<expr>** can be recursive as one possibility for **<exp3>** is a complete **<expr>** enclosed in brackets.

Sets of BNF rules are not the only convenient way to specify the syntax of a language. This can also be done as a set of syntax diagrams. The equivalent specification expressed diagrammatically would appear as follows with rectangular boxes enclosing items for which further syntax diagrams exist and rounded boxes enclosing items to be typed as shown.

The two forms of specification are exactly equivalent but some people picture the situation better with syntax diagrams than with BNF rules and vice versa:

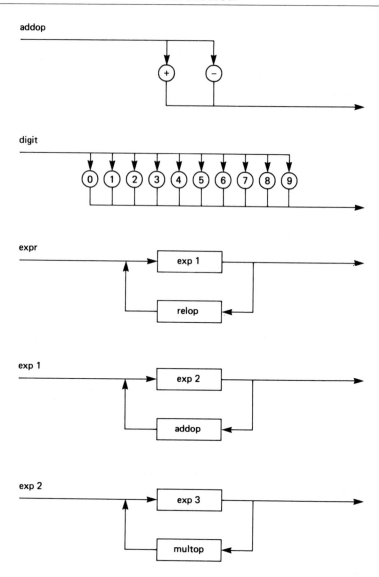

exp 3

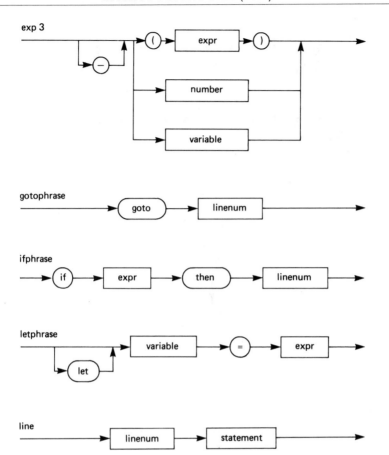

gotophrase

ifphrase

letphrase

line

letter

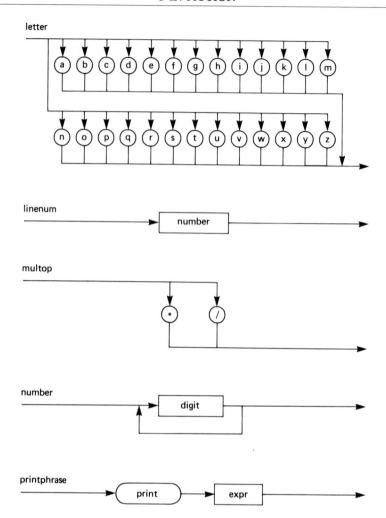

linenum

number

multop

* /

number

digit

printphrase

print   expr

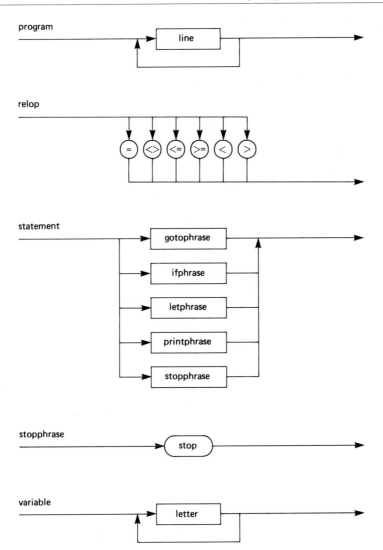

16.3 COMPILER OUTPUT

Now that you have a complete syntax specification for the source language it is time to look at the output you will expect from the compiler. In practice for any particular source language that you may want to compile there is an ideal machine code into which it can most easily and most efficiently be translated. Unfortunately it is unlikely that any real processor exists with the ideal machine code as its assembly language. But this is a problem I shall tackle in Chapter 17. For now I shall be content to describe an ideal machine code for TINY BASIC translation and write a compiler to translate TINY BASIC source into it. Any ideal machine language for TINY BASIC translation purposes must be able to deal effectively with expressions, as this seems to be the basis of the language.

For example, the three main action statements are IF, LET and PRINT, and execution of all three is based on expression evaluation.

To execute an IF statement you evaluate the expression and if the result is non-zero branch to a given line number.

To execute a LET statement you evaluate the expression to the right of the = and then assign the result to the specified variable.

To execute a PRINT statement you evaluate the following expression and then output the result to the terminal.

As you can see, all three follow the same pattern with just a different action to perform with the result at the end of expression evaluation.

One of the most effective ways to evaluate expressions is to translate them into a slightly different form called **reverse Polish notation** (RPN). With RPN the operators are placed after the two operands to which they refer instead of between them.

For example, the expression:

a+b

would become the RPN expression:

a b +

and the ordinary expression:

(a+b)*c

would become the RPN expression:

a b + c *

The advantage of using RPN is that after translation there are no brackets to consider and no operator precedence rules to work on. Both of these things are taken care of by the translation process. A further advantage is that RPN expression evaluation is very simple, using a stack to store intermediate results. In fact only two simple rules need to be used to evaluate an RPN expression in a single left to right pass through the symbols:

1. When an operand is encountered push its value on to the stack;
2. When an operator is encountered, pop the number of operands off the stack that the operator requires, apply the operator to these operands and then push the result back on to the stack.

Using these rules the result of the expression will be found on top of the stack at the end of the evaluation. For example:

(2+3)*4

translated to RPN becomes:

2 3 + 4 *

Scanning this RPN expression left to right the first symbol encountered is the operand value 2. Applying rule 1, this value is pushed on to the stack. The next symbol is the operand value 3 which is also stacked by rule 1. Next the addition operator is encountered. This is a binary operator meaning that it takes two operands and by rule 2, the two operands (3 and 2) are popped off the stack and added together to give a result of 5, which is then returned to the empty stack. The next symbol is the operand value 4 which is stacked on top of the 5 that is already there. Finally, the binary multiply operator takes its two operands off the stack, multiplies them together and returns the end result (20) to the otherwise empty stack as expected.

A simple list of instructions that give the sequence of steps to follow to evaluate the expression are:

get number 2
get number 3
addition
get number 4
multiplication

This sequence can be further abbreviated to give a set of instructions that look remarkably like machine code as follows:

getnm 2
getnm 3
addn
getnm 4
mult

The definition of the **getnm** instruction is that it takes the value of its operand and pushes it on to the machine stack. The instructions **addn** and **mult** each take the top two stack entries, perform their operation on the two values and return the result to the stack.

The complete list of ideal machine code instructions needed for expression evaluation using this method is:

getnm — Stacks its numeric operand value
fetch — Stacks its variable operand value
addn ⎫
subn ⎪   Perform the standard four
mult ⎬   mathematical functions
divn ⎭
tsteq — Test for equal
tstne — Test for not equal
tstle — Test for less than or equal to
tstge — Test for greater than or equal to
tstlt — Test for less than
tstgt — Test for greater than
minus — Unary minus

So the ordinary expression:

x+y>9

translates to RPN as:

x y + 9 >

This can now further be translated into the ideal machine code sequence:

```
fetch x
fetch y
addn
getnm 9
tstgt
```

Once expressions can be translated then translating full statements is easy. An IF statement requires an extra instruction I shall call JUMP with a line number label as its operand. What this instruction does is to remove the top stack entry and if the value is non-zero (i.e. TRUE) cause a branch to the specified line label. This means that the statement:

if x=6 then 50

would translate to the sequence:

```
fetch x
getnm 6
tsteq
jump 50
```

The LET statement can also be translated by the addition of a single new instruction called STORE. What the instruction does is to take the top of stack value and store it in the specified variable so that for example the line:

let x=y−9

would translate to:

```
fetch y
getnm 9
subn
store x
```

The PRINT statement is the same as the LET and IF statements except that its extra instruction (PRINT) takes the top of stack value and sends it to your terminal as printable characters. So that:

print −a

becomes the sequence:

```
fetch a
minus
print
```

Minus is slightly different from the other operators in that it is a UNARY operator and so only takes one operand. In RPN evaluation terms this means that minus takes the top stack entry, multiplies it by −1 to negate the value and returns the result to the stack as usual.

The only things you do not yet know how to translate are GOTO and STOP statements. The action of these two statements is so elementary that these statements can be their own machine code instructions.

You should now be able to hand compile simple TINY BASIC programs into ideal machine code. Take a break for a while and have a go at this one:

```
10 let x = 0
20 if x = 10 then 60
30 print x
40 x = x+1
50 goto 20
60 stop
```

Remember that the first stage on any line containing an expression is to translate the expression into RPN. You should also use the new machine code instruction LABEL to deal with the line numbers at the start of each line.

The solution appears as follows:

```
label 10
getnm 0
store x
label 20
fetch x
getnm 10
tsteq
jump 60
label 30
fetch x
print
label 40
fetch x
getnm 1
addn
store x
label 50
goto 20
label 60
stop
```

If your answer is different from this one, try going back to take another look at the section that is causing you problems.

16.4 RECURSIVE DESCENT

You have now seen the definition of the TINY BASIC source code and the ideal machine code into which it will be translated. You have also looked at the translation process itself for getting from one to the other. All that remains now is to automate the process by writing a C program that can perform the translation task.

Notice at this point how much thought and discussion have gone on to get to the stage you are at now — not a single line of code has been written yet, and this is just as it should be!

However, the title of this section is not intended to give the impression that you are now over the hill and on the way down the other side. Recursive descent is a method (one of many) for writing programs that can parse the syntax of a language, given a formal syntax specification for the language. You already have such a syntax specification for TINY BASIC in the form of the BNF rules you studied earlier.

In order to use recursive descent all you have to do is look at each of the rules in turn, starting with <**program**> and write small modules of code that can deal with each of them in turn. The BNF specification says that a <**program**> is a sequence of <**line**> and that each <**line**> is a <**linenum**> followed by a <**statement**>. Writing these requirements into a sort of semi-English program (called pseudo-code) gives:

```
while getting a <line> != EOF
    translate <linenum>
    check for <statement> keywords and
    translate the given <statement>
```

What this says is: repeatedly get lines until there are no lines left, and for each line translate its line number and then the statement contained on the line. As you can see, this is rather like a cross between a programming language and English, and it is very useful for setting down initial thoughts on paper. At this point you should be convinced that the 'getting a <**line**>' bit and the 'translate <**linenum**>' bit are both very straightforward and can both be performed by simple C functions. The more difficult part is sorting out which of the five statement keywords is present on the line and then dealing with the translation of that keyword. The next refinement step then ought to be an expansion of that part of the pseudo-code program. The BNF specification says that <**statement**> is one of <**gotophrase**>, <**ifphrase**>, <**letphrase**>, <**printphrase**> or <**stopphrase**>. This indicates some sort of five-way branch to five separate routines each of which can deal with one of the five <**statement**> types:

```
while getting a line != EOF
    translate <linenum>
    if <statement> ==goto
        do <gotophrase>
    else if <statement> ==if
        do <ifphrase>
    else if <statement> ==let
        do <letphrase>
    else if <statement> ==print
        do <printphrase>
    else if <statement> ==stop
        do <stopphrase>
    else
        do <letphrase>
```

Notice that it is possible for there to be none of the five statement keywords on a given line and for the line still to be valid. This is because the LET keyword in a <**letphrase**> is optional. As a result, the default action at the end of the multiple **if** construct assumes a <letphrase> without a LET. At this stage it should be possible to write the first bit of C code towards the program by a straight translation of the pseudo-code that I have built up. To make this process easier I will use a call to an (as yet) unwritten C function wherever I encounter an item whose BNF rule I have not yet considered. The C code therefore becomes:

```
main()
{
        while (getline())
        {
                linenum();
                if (check("let"))
                        dolet();
                else if (check("print"))
                        doprint();
                else if (check("if"))
                        doif();
                else if (check("goto"))
                        dogoto();
                else if (check("stop"))
                        dostop();
                else
                        dolet();
        }
}
```

Having used some C functions, now is a good time to sort out the input, output and functional specifications for them.

The **getline()** function is replacing the pseudo-code instruction 'getting a line != EOF'. In order to meet that description and to provide a value that can be tested as a **while** condition, the **getline()** function needs to be able to read a line of text up to a new line (\n) or EOF character and return a zero value when the line of text read is empty. When a line of text is read that does contain characters, **getline()** should return a non-zero (TRUE) value so that the line can be processed within the while loop. Obviously as **getline()** is reading characters it needs to store them into some sort of buffer so that other functions may access the text lines. An array of **char** is most suitable for this and the global definitions:

#define MAXLINE 256
char inbuf[MAXLINE];

can be added to the program.

The **linenum()** function has the job of looking at the text in **inbuf[]** and extracting the line number from the start of the line. You already know that the ideal machine code I have defined uses the instruction LABEL to mark line number positions, so **linenum()** needs to generate a LABEL instruction followed, as an operand, by the line number encountered on the line. In order to carry out this job, **linenum()** will need some sort of pointer to the start of the line which can be advanced along the characters of the line number as they are accepted. The same pointer can then be left pointing to a position on the line just beyond the line number to tell other functions where to begin their tasks. This will add a further global definition:

char *bufptr;

The **check()** function is going to be used to look for a given string of characters starting at the current **bufptr** position within the text line. If the string given as a parameter is not the next thing on the line then **check()** will return a zero (FALSE) value. If the string is the next thing on the line then check will step **bufptr** beyond the matched text, ready for the next function, and return a non-zero (TRUE) value.

The functions **dolet()**, **doprint()**, **doif()**, **dogoto()** and **dostop()** will each examine the rest of the text line starting at the **bufptr** position and generate ideal machine code sequences from the source code. By reference to the BNF rules and the function specifications just presented all the functions discussed can now be written:

```
getline()
{
        int c,i;

        bufptr = inbuf;

        for (i = 0; (c = getchar()) != '\n' && c != EOF; i++)
                inbuf[i] = c;

        inbuf[i] = '\0';

        return((i == 0) ? 0 : 1);
}
```

As you can see, **getline()** copies text from the standard input into **inbuf[]** one character at a time. At the end of the line a **\0** terminator is added. If there is no text to process in **inbuf[]** then **getline** returns the value 0, otherwise 1 is returned.

Looking now at **linenum()**, the BNF rules say that < **linenum** > is a < **number** > and that < **number** > is a sequence of one or more < **digit** > characters (0–9). The function specification also says that **linenum()** has to generate a LABEL instruction. Combining these two parts gives the **linenum()** function as:

```
linenum()
{
        printf("label ");

        while (*bufptr >= '0' && *bufptr <= '9')
                printf("%c",*bufptr++);

        printf("\n");
}
```

The next function, **check()**, is easy to write as specified. However, I need to complicate it slightly to take spaces into account. In TINY BASIC there are no restrictions specified as to the number of spaces that may appear between items on a line (as long as the overall length of a line does not exceed MAXLINE). Syntactically the spaces are not required, they just aid human readability. This means that the compiler needs to ignore them. This could be done by having a function to step over blanks on a line and calling the function whenever spaces might be encountered. A simpler way is to incorporate the job of that function into **check()**, which will now step over all spaces before and after the string for which it checks:

```
check(ptr)
char *ptr;
{
        char *tptr;

        while (*bufptr == ' ')
                bufptr++;

        tptr = bufptr;

        while (*ptr != '\0' && *ptr == *tptr)
        {
                ptr++;
                tptr++;
        }

        if (*ptr != '\0')
                return(0);
        else
        {
                bufptr = tptr;
                while (*bufptr == ' ')
                        bufptr++;
                return(1);
        }
}
```

As the number of functions increases you ought to be giving consideration to splitting them up into separate files containing related groups of functions. These groupings should not be considered as static and unchanging — a function which seems appropriately grouped at one time may need to be moved later as more functions are written and more natural groupings appear.

For this program I have chosen four groupings — the first called **main.c**, contains the functions **main()** (and because they are only called from **main()**, **getline()** and **linenum()**).

The second group called **stmt.c** will contain **doprint()**, **dolet()**, **doif()**, **dogoto()** and **dostop()** that deal with the five TINY BASIC statements.

The third group called **util.c** will contain **check()** and any other general utility functions that will be called from different places.

The final group called **expr.c** will deal with the expression evaluation functions when I get round to them.

The five statement functions can now be written into **stmt.c**. Remember that by the time the statement functions are called, the keywords to which they refer have already been dealt with in the function **main()**.

Taking the simplest function first, you should see that **dostop()** has only to generate a STOP instruction and then a new line (\n) character as follows:

```
dostop()
{
        printf("stop\n");
}
```

The next simplest function is **doprint()**. The BNF rule for **<print-phrase>** says it is the keyword PRINT followed by a numeric expression **<expr>**. Translating this to ideal machine code involves dealing with the expression then following this with a PRINT instruction. Dealing with expressions is something that needs to be done in several other places as well as **doprint()**, so a function will be used to give:

```
doprint()
{
        expr();
        printf("print\n");
}
```

The TINY BASIC GOTO statement (**<gotophrase>**) consists of the keyword GOTO followed by a **<linenum>** which itself is a sequence of **<digit>** s.

```
dogoto()
{
        printf("goto ");

        while (*bufptr >= '0' && *bufptr <= '9')
                printf("%c",*bufptr++);

        printf("\n");
}
```

The LET statement is translated as an expression followed by a STORE instruction. The BNF rule for **<letphrase>** gives **<variable>** followed by an equals sign followed by **<expr>**. This can be coded as:

```
dolet()
{
        char *varptr;

        varptr = bufptr;
        while (*bufptr++ != '=');
        *(bufptr-1) = '\0';
        expr();
        printf("store %s\n",varptr);
}
```

Notice that syntactically the <**variable**> occurs at the start of a <**letphrase**> but in translation the STORE instruction that uses the variable name occurs at the end. This is the reason for the variable **varptr**, it is used to mark the start of the variable name which is then printed as the operand to the STORE instruction.

The final function in this group is **doif()**. Notice that the syntax of the IF statement requires the use of the word THEN between the <**expr**> and the <**linenum**>. This is dealt with by a call to a function named **scan()**. The **scan()** function does a similar job to **check()** except that if a match is not found an error message is printed and program execution terminates.

```
doif()
{
        expr();
        scan("then");
        printf("jump ");

        while (*bufptr >= '0' && *bufptr <= '9')
                printf("%c",*bufptr++);

        printf("\n");
}
```

As the **scan()** function performs a similar task to **check()** it can be coded using **check()** and stored in **util.c** along with **check()**.

```
scan(ptr)
char *ptr;
{
        if (check(ptr))
                return(1);

        printf("Syntax error\n");
        exit(1);
}
```

All that remains now is to sort out **expr()**. As before I shall code this by direct reference to the BNF rules as required by the recursive descent method. <**expr**> is defined to be <**exp1**> optionally repeatedly followed by a <**relop**> and another <**exp1**>. This gives the following code for the function **expr()**:

```
expr()
{
        exp1();

        for (;;)
                if (check("=")) {
                        exp1(); printf("tsteq\n"); }
                else if (check("<>")) {
                        exp1(); printf("tstne\n"); }
                else if (check("<=")) {
                        exp1(); printf("tstle\n"); }
                else if (check(">=")) {
                        exp1(); printf("tstge\n"); }
                else if (check("<")) {
                        exp1(); printf("tstlt\n"); }
                else if (check(">")) {
                        exp1(); printf("tstgt\n"); }
                else
                        return;
}
```

Remember that <**relop**> is one of =, < >, <=, >=, < or > and notice that each of these cases is explicitly checked for by this function. This makes the translation to RPN an automatic by-product of the syntax analysis.

The other functions that need to be written are **exp1()** called from **expr()**, **exp2()** which will be called from **exp1()** in a similar way and **exp3()** which will be called from **exp2()**. Finally, **exp3()** will call three functions as per the BNF rule for <**exp3**>. One will be a recursive call to **expr()** if a bracketed sub-expression is encountered and the other two will be **getnum()** and **getvar()** to sort out the BNF constructs <**number**> and <**variable**> respectively. This will give an overall set of functions and files that look as follows:

```
/*
:::::::::::::::::::
main.c
:::::::::::::::::::
*/


#include <stdio.h>

#define MAXLINE 256

char *bufptr, inbuf[MAXLINE];

main()
{
        while (getline())
        {
                linenum();
                if (check("let"))
                        dolet();
                else if (check("print"))
                        doprint();
                else if (check("if"))
                        doif();
                else if (check("stop"))
                        dostop();
                else if (check("goto"))
                        dogoto();
                else
                        dolet();
        }
        printf("\n");
}


getline()
{
        int c,i;

        bufptr = inbuf;

        for (i = 0; (c = getchar()) != '\n' && c != EOF; i++)
                inbuf[i] = c;

        inbuf[i] = '\0';

        return((i == 0) ? 0 : 1);
}


linenum()
{
        printf("label ");

        while (*bufptr >= '0' && *bufptr <= '9')
                printf("%c",*bufptr++);

        printf("\n");
}
```

```
/*
::::::::::::::::::
stmt.c
::::::::::::::::::
*/

#include <stdio.h>

#define MAXLINE 256

extern char *bufptr, inbuf[MAXLINE];

doprint()
{
        expr();
        printf("print\n");
}


dolet()
{
        char *varptr;

        varptr = bufptr;
        while (*bufptr++ != '=');
        *(bufptr-1) = '\0';
        expr();
        printf("store %s\n",varptr);
}


doif()
{
        expr();
        scan("then");
        printf("jump ");

        while (*bufptr >= '0' && *bufptr <= '9')
                printf("%c",*bufptr++);

        printf("\n");
}


dostop()
{
        printf("stop\n");
}


dogoto()
{
        printf("goto ");

        while (*bufptr >= '0' && *bufptr <= '9')
                printf("%c",*bufptr++);

        printf("\n");
}
```

```
/*
:::::::::::::::::::::
expr.c
:::::::::::::::::::::
*/

#include <stdio.h>

#define MAXLINE 256

extern char *bufptr, inbuf[MAXLINE];

expr()
{
        exp1();

        for (;;)
                if (check("=")) {
                        exp1(); printf("tsteq\n"); }
                else if (check("<>")) {
                        exp1(); printf("tstne\n"); }
                else if (check("<=")) {
                        exp1(); printf("tstle\n"); }
                else if (check(">=")) {
                        exp1(); printf("tstge\n"); }
                else if (check("<")) {
                        exp1(); printf("tstlt\n"); }
                else if (check(">")) {
                        exp1(); printf("tstgt\n"); }
                else
                        return;
}


exp1()
{
        exp2();

        for (;;)
                if (check("+")) {
                        exp2(); printf("addn\n"); }
                else if (check("-")) {
                        exp2(); printf("subn\n"); }
                else
                        return;
}


exp2()
{
        exp3();

        for (;;)
                if (check("*")) {
                        exp3(); printf("mult\n"); }
                else if (check("/")) {
                        exp3(); printf("divn\n"); }
                else
                        return;
}
```

```
/*
::::::::::::::::::::::
expr.c - cont...
::::::::::::::::::::::
*/


exp3()
{
        int s;

        s = (check("-")) ? -1 : 1;

        if (check("("))
        {
                expr();
                scan(")");
        }
        else
                if (*bufptr >= '0' && *bufptr <= '9')
                        getnum();
                else
                        getvar();

        if (s == -1)
                printf("minus\n");
}


getnum()
{
        printf("getnm ");

        while (*bufptr >= '0' && *bufptr <= '9')
                printf("%c",*bufptr++);

        printf("\n");
}


getvar()
{
        if (*bufptr < 'a' || *bufptr > 'z') {
                printf("Syntax error\n");
                exit(1);
        }

        printf("fetch ");

        while (*bufptr >= 'a' && *bufptr <= 'z')
                printf("%c",*bufptr++);

        printf("\n");
}
```

```
/*
::::::::::::::::::::
util.c
::::::::::::::::::::
*/

#include <stdio.h>

#define MAXLINE 256

extern char *bufptr, inbuf[MAXLINE];

check(ptr)
char *ptr;
{
        char *tptr;

        while (*bufptr == ' ')
                bufptr++;

        tptr = bufptr;

        while (*ptr != '\0' && *ptr == *tptr)
        {
                ptr++;
                tptr++;
        }

        if (*ptr != '\0')
                return(0);
        else
        {
                bufptr = tptr;
                while (*bufptr == ' ')
                        bufptr++;
                return(1);
        }
}


scan(ptr)
char *ptr;
{
        if (check(ptr))
                return(1);

        printf("Syntax error\n");
        exit(1);
}
```

All that remains now is to simplify the compilation and maintenance process with the creation of a suitable MAKEFILE as follows:

```
bcom:    main.o stmt.o expr.o util.o
         cc main.o stmt.o expr.o util.o -o bcom

main.o:  main.c
         cc -c main.c

stmt.o:  stmt.c
         cc -c stmt.c

expr.o:  expr.c
         cc -c expr.c

util.o:  util.c
         cc -c util.c
```

Having got any typing errors out of the files and finally made the suite of programs compile, you should create a suitable BASIC source file such as:

```
10 a = 10
20 let b = 20
30 c = 30
40 if a*b >= 12*c then 80
50 print -a-5
60 a = a+1
70 goto 40
80 print a*a
90 stop
```

If you call this source file **test.bas** then the command line:

$ bcom <test.bas >test.rpn

should translate the contents of the file **test.bas** into ideal machine code and send the result to the file **test.rpn** as follows:

```
label 10
getnm 10
store a
label 20
getnm 20
store b
label 30
getnm 30
store c
label 40
fetch a
fetch b
mult
getnm 12
fetch c
mult
tstge
jump 80
label 50
fetch a
minus
getnm 5
subn
print
label 60
fetch a
getnm 1
addn
store a
label 70
goto 40
label 80
fetch a
fetch a
mult
print
label 90
stop
```

The shell in action

The work you have seen so far on the TINY BASIC compiler has been quite general — it takes TINY BASIC source code and translates it into the ideal machine code I defined. Unfortunately, there is no real processor that uses this machine code as its assembly language (none I know of anyway). So even though the compiler demonstrates some valuable principles it is not of much practical value. Unless, that is, some method can be found to execute the ideal machine code programs. That is the subject of this chapter.

There are many methods of achieving this objective. I shall briefly present three of them and then look at one in more detail, ending up with a program that produces executable code.

17.1 EXECUTING IDEAL MACHINE CODE

The most obvious way to execute the output from the TINY BASIC compiler is to write a simple interpreter that knows how to perform the required action for each of the ideal machine code instructions. There are several commercially available compilers based upon this technique. One is called the UCSD-P system. The P stands for pseudo-code because this is the name given to the ideal machine code generated by the compilers. It is a fairly straightforward task to develop compilers for several different source languages that all use the same P-code. This means that once a P-code interpreter has been written for any particular machine, any of the available compilers can be used without any further work. Obviously this method of porting compilers from one machine to another requires that the compilers themselves are supplied as P-code programs so that they too can be run by the P-code interpreter.

Another technique that is often used in small compilers is that a set of subroutines is written in the target machine's own native machine code, such that each ideal machine code instruction has a subroutine to perform its actions. This set of subroutines is known as the 'run-time library' as it is only required when programs are run. The ideal machine code programs are then translated into a set of native machine code subroutine call instructions to the appropriate run-time library subroutines. Any operands to an ideal machine code instruction can be passed to the run-time library routine in an appropriate manner. This usually means either on the machine stack or in processor registers.

The third method is similar to the second in that a native code routine is written to deal with each ideal machine code instruction. The difference, however, is that these routines are used like templates rather than subroutines. This means that whenever a particular ideal machine code instruction is encountered in a program the native code routine is substituted for that instruction. This is rather like the substitutions that take place with **#define** macro definitions in C programs. Any operand values for a given ideal machine code instruction are actually used to modify the native code template before substitution takes place.

Using the third method always generates faster executing code than the second method, even if the same routines are used for both, as there is no overhead in instructions or time for the subroutine calls or the return instructions at the end of each subroutine. The third method can even generate shorter code if the individual template routines are themselves short. However, if the individual templates are quite long then it wastes a lot of program space to have to substitute repeatedly in a long routine.

A practical translator can be produced which combines the best features of both methods two and three. This translator will use subroutines and subroutine calls whenever the native code for a particular ideal machine code instruction is long, thus saving space. Whenever the native code is short, however, then a template/macro will be used for speed.

The next thing to do is to write a set of native code routines to perform the actions of each of the ideal machine code instructions. Before this can be done, however, a fundamental decision needs to be made — on which processor are the native code routines to run?

17.2 THE Z80 ARCHITECTURE AND INSTRUCTION SET

The choice of processor is not really important; the principles remain the same whichever choice is made. However, the Z80 is a simple processor that does not have built-in instructions for multiply and divide. This means that software routines need to be written to perform these functions. And these routines will be large enough to implement as subroutines rather than templates — an important point for a demonstration program.

Obviously, you may not be familiar with the Z80 so I shall need to digress for a short time to discuss some things you will find helpful. If you are already familiar with the Z80 instruction set and register set then you will not miss anything if you skip to the next section (17.3).

The Z80 contains 22 internal registers that are directly accessible to the programmer. Some of these are general purpose and others have special functions to perform. Only eight of these registers will be used in the translator. They are shown in Fig. 17.1.

Both 8-bit and 16-bit operations can be performed on the Z80. The 8-bit operations use the 8-bit registers A, F, B, C, D, E, H and L. The A register has a special function as the 8-bit accumulator. This is the register into which all

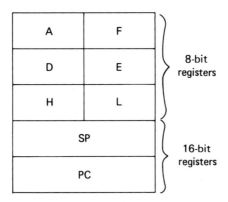

Fig. 17.1 Simplified Z80 register set

the 8-bit arithmetic and logical instructions accumulate their results. The F register also has a special function; it contains a set of single bit flags that are used to indicate useful information about the results of previously executed instructions. In particular two of the flags are very important. The Z (zero) flag is set whenever the result of the previous arithmetic or logical operation produced a zero value. The other useful flag, the C (carry) flag, is set whenever a previous addition or subtraction operation resulted in a carry or a borrow being generated. As you will see, special instructions are available which can test the state of these flags and cause a branch to some other part of the program depending upon the results.

The 16-bit registers are: PC which is the program counter and is used to point to the next instruction to execute. A program branch instruction works just by loading the PC register with a new value showing where program execution is to continue. The register SP is the Z80 stack pointer; there are special instructions which can **PUSH** and **POP** 16-bit values on to and off the stack. These instructions automatically update the contents of SP so that it always points to the top of the stack in memory. In addition to this it is also possible to treat particular pairs of 8-bit registers as though they were 16-bit registers. The pairs are AF, BC, DE and HL. When used for 16-bit work the HL register pair takes on the role of 16-bit accumulator.

The parts of the instruction set that you will see in the translator and the functions performed are:

LD A,H	Loads the accumulator with the 8-bit value in H
LD A,6	Loads the accumulator with the immediate value 6
OR L	Performs 8-bit logical OR operation of the L register into the accumulator
JP Z,L600	Jump if the zero flag is set to label L600
JP NZ,L500	Jump if the zero flag is reset to label L500
CALL L400	Jump to a subroutine starting at label L400 and PUSH a return address on to the stack
PUSH HL	Put the contents of the HL register pair on to the stack and modify SP ready for the next stack operation
POP DE	Take the top entry from the stack and copy it into DE
LD HL, (VA)	Load HL with a 16-bit value that starts at address VA
LD (VB),HL	Load a 16-bit value into memory starting at address VB from the contents of HL
EX DE,HL	Exchange the contents of the 16-bit register pairs DE and HL

This is not an exhaustive list of all the instructions used but an example of each instruction type is given.

17.3 THE TEMPLATE LIBRARY

The next task is to work out a set of templates, one for each ideal machine code instruction.

17.3.1 fetch var

This takes the contents of the given variable (var) and **PUSH**es the value on to the stack. In Z80 assembly code this gives:

```
LD HL, (var)
PUSH HL
```

Whenever a **fetch** instruction is encountered the translator should replace it with these two Z80 assembly code instructions. Notice that whatever variable name occurs as an operand to the **fetch** instruction, it should be copied into the brackets of the first Z80 instruction. You will see that for all the ideal machine code instructions with operands there will be a place within the corresponding Z80 template for the operand to fit in. And it will be part of the translator's task to fit the operands into the appropriate positions.

17.3.2 store var

This **POP**s the value off the top of the stack and stores it in the specified variable (**var**).

```
POP HL
LD (var),HL
```

17.3.3 getnm num

This takes the specified operand value (**num**) and **PUSH**es the value on to the stack.

```
LD HL,num
PUSH HL
```

17.3.4 jump line

This takes the top value from the stack and tests it for zero. If the value is non-zero (TRUE) then a jump is made to the specified line label.

```
POP HL
LD A,H
OR L
JP NZ,line
```

This code requires a little explanation as it is not quite as obvious as the others. First the top of stack value is **POP**ped into HL. At this point the value in HL needs to be tested for a zero value. Unfortunately there is no simple Z80 instruction to perform this test. To overcome this problem the HL register pair is treated as two 8-bit values in H and L. These two values are logical ORed together with the result appearing in the accumulator (A register). If HL contains a zero value to start with then ORing H and L together will leave zero in A. Any other starting value in HL will leave a non-zero value in A. In addition to the result in A the flags will also be affected, in particular the zero (Z) flag will be set if A ends up with a zero value. The final instruction uses a conditional jump to test the value of the zero flag for the non-zero (NZ) condition. Remember a non-zero value in A means that HL contains a non-zero (TRUE) value and the jump will be taken to the given line label as required.

17.3.5 goto line

This performs an unconditional jump to the given line label.

```
JP label
```

None of the other ideal machine code instructions requires an operand so they are more straightforward to translate than those you have seen so far.

17.3.6 addn

This takes the top two stack entries, adds them together and returns the result to the top of the stack:

```
POP HL
POP DE
ADD HL,DE
PUSH HL
```

This routine is very simple. However, the subtract routine is not quite so easy.

17.3.7 subn

This subtracts the top of stack value from the next on stack value and returns the result to the stack:

```
POP DE
POP HL
OR A
SBC HL,DE
PUSH HL
```

Notice that with subtract it matters which value gets subtracted from which. The Z80 16-bit subtract instruction subtracts DE from HL so the values need to be **POP**ped in the right order. A quirk of the Z80 instruction set is that 16-bit subtraction can only be done involving the carry flag as well.

This means that the contents of the carry flag get subtracted from HL as well as the value in DE. In order that this does not present a problem, it is necessary to ensure that the carry flag contains a zero value before the subtract operation takes place. At this point yet another quirk of the Z80 instruction set creeps into the story — there is no 'reset the carry flag' instruction (it can be set (SCF) and complemented (CCF) but not reset). In order to perform this operation it is usual to use a side-effect of another instruction. The side-effect is that all of the logical instructions reset the carry flag. The one logical instruction that does not otherwise do anything useful is OR A, as ORing the accumulator with itself leaves the value in A unchanged! As you can see therefore, the OR A instruction does nothing but reset the carry flag — just what is needed. (I think that the OR A instruction might more profitably have been called RCF, however . . . .)

At this point, you have enough templates available to be able to hand translate a line of TINY BASIC source right through to Z80 assembly code. Try the following:

let y=x+3

Translating this to ideal machine code gives:

```
fetch x
getnm 3
addn
store y
```

Each of these instructions can now be substituted for a template from the ones you have just seen:

```
LD HL,(x)
PUSH HL
LD HL,3
PUSH HL
POP HL
POP DE
ADD HL,DE
PUSH HL
POP HL
LD (y),HL
```

Notice that just blindly substituting the templates for ideal machine code instructions leads to the inclusion in the final code of two pairs of redundant **PUSH HL/POP HL** instructions. Our translator is more sophisticated than this and will include code optimization to remove these redundant instructions so leaving the code:

```
LD HL,(x)
PUSH HL
LD HL,3
POP DE
ADD HL,DE
LD (y),HL
```

In fact, a really good translator would optimize this code still further to give:

```
LD HL,(x)
LD DE,3
ADD HL,DE
LD (y),HL
```

But our translator will not be this sophisticated; it will stop at the previous stage, having removed the redundant **PUSH HL/POP HL** instruction pairs. The simplest way to remove these redundant instructions during translation is not to **PUSH HL** at the end of a template but to flag the fact that there is a significant value in HL instead. Then at the start of the next template, if a value is required in HL no further action need be taken as the value is already flagged as present. If at the start of the next template a significant value in HL is not required, but one is flagged as present, then HL can be **PUSH**ed on to the stack knowing that it will not immediately be **POP**ped off again.

The templates for the rest of the ideal machine code instructions are quite straightforward and are left as an exercise for you to work out from the full translator listing given. All the rest of the binary operator instructions (**mult**, **divn**, **tsteq**, **tstne**, etc.) and the **PRINT** instruction are sufficiently complex that they are best implemented as subroutines rather than completely as templates/macros. The template part of these instructions just sets up the correct values in HL and DE and then arranges a **CALL** to the appropriate subroutine. Whenever a subroutine **CALL** instruction is generated, a flag is set so that at the end of the program translation, those subroutines that have been **CALL**ed can be included on the end of the Z80 code.

17.4 THE TRANSLATOR

Knowing what the input to the translator looks like and knowing what the output will be, it is a simple task to write a shell script to do the job.

Essentially the program consists of a **WHILE** loop which will be used to **READ** lines of ideal machine code from the standard input into two shell variables (**CMD** and **PARAM**). A shell script **CASE** statement can then be used, based on the value of the first variable to branch to a set of separate routines to deal with the translation of individual instructions. The asterisk *) **CASE** is the one that gets executed at the end of the input file and which sorts out the inclusion of any necessary subroutines. A few extra lines of code have also been added to the translator so that the ideal machine code instructions are embedded in the translator output as comments.

```
FLAG=FALSE
DIV=FALSE
MUL=FALSE
PRT=FALSE
TST=FALSE
EQ=0
NE=1
LE=2
GE=3
LT=4
GT=5
while read CMD PARAM
do
    echo ";"
    echo "; $CMD $PARAM"
    case $CMD in
        fetch)  if test $FLAG = TRUE
                then
                            echo "        PUSH    HL"
                fi
                echo "        LD      HL,(v$PARAM)"
                FLAG=TRUE
                ;;
        store)  if test $FLAG = FALSE
                then
                            echo "        POP     HL"
                fi
                echo "        LD      (v$PARAM),HL"
                FLAG=FALSE
                ;;
        getnm)  if test $FLAG = TRUE
                then
                            echo "        PUSH    HL"
                fi
                echo "        LD      HL,$PARAM"
                FLAG=TRUE
                ;;
        jump)   if test $FLAG = FALSE
                then
                            echo "        POP     HL"
                fi
                echo "        LD      A,H"
                echo "        OR      L"
                echo "        JP      NZ,L$PARAM"
                FLAG=FALSE
                ;;
```

```
print)   if test $FLAG = FALSE
         then
                     echo "          POP       HL"
         fi
         echo "          CALL      PRINT"
         FLAG=FALSE
         PRT=TRUE
         ;;
goto)    echo "          JP        L$PARAM"
         ;;
stop)    echo "          HALT"
         ;;
tsteq)   if test $FLAG = FALSE
         then
                     echo "          POP       HL"
         fi
         echo "          POP       DE"
         echo "          LD        A,$EQ"
         echo "          CALL      TEST"
         FLAG=TRUE
         TST=TRUE
         ;;
tstne)   if test $FLAG = FALSE
         then
                     echo "          POP       HL"
         fi
         echo "          POP       DE"
         echo "          LD        A,$NE"
         echo "          CALL      TEST"
         FLAG=TRUE
         TST=TRUE
         ;;
tstle)   if test $FLAG = FALSE
         then
                     echo "          POP       HL"
         fi
         echo "          POP       DE"
         echo "          LD        A,$LE"
         echo "          CALL      TEST"
         FLAG=TRUE
         TST=TRUE
         ;;
tstge)   if test $FLAG = FALSE
         then
                     echo "          POP       HL"
         fi
         echo "          POP       DE"
         echo "          LD        A,$GE"
         echo "          CALL      TEST"
         FLAG=TRUE
         TST=TRUE
         ;;
tstlt)   if test $FLAG = FALSE
         then
                     echo "          POP       HL"
         fi
         echo "          POP       DE"
         echo "          LD        A,$LT"
         echo "          CALL      TEST"
         FLAG=TRUE
         TST=TRUE
         ;;
tstgt)   if test $FLAG = FALSE
         then
```

```
                    echo "            POP       HL"
          fi
          echo "            POP       DE"
          echo "            LD        A,$GT"
          echo "            CALL      TEST"
          FLAG=TRUE
          TST=TRUE
          ;;
addn)     if test $FLAG = FALSE
          then
                    echo "            POP       HL"
          fi
          echo "            POP       DE"
          echo "            ADD       HL,DE"
          FLAG=TRUE
          ;;
subn)     if test $FLAG = TRUE
          then
                    echo "            EX        DE,HL"
          else
                    echo "            POP       DE"
          fi
          echo "            POP       HL"
          echo "            OR        A"
          echo "            SBC       HL,DE"
          FLAG=TRUE
          ;;
mult)     if test $FLAG = FALSE
          then
                    echo "            POP       HL"
          fi
          echo "            POP       DE"
          echo "            CALL      MULT"
          FLAG=TRUE
          MUL=TRUE
          ;;
divn)     if test $FLAG = TRUE
          then
                    echo "            EX        DE,HL"
          else
                    echo "            POP       DE"
          fi
          echo "            POP       HL"
          echo "            CALL      DIVN"
          FLAG=TRUE
          DIV=TRUE
          ;;
minus)    if test $FLAG = FALSE
          then
                    echo "            POP       HL"
          fi
          echo "            LD        A,H"
          echo "            CPL"
          echo "            LD        H,A"
          echo "            LD        A,L"
          echo "            CPL"
          echo "            LD        L,A"
          echo "            INC       HL"
          FLAG=TRUE
          ;;
label)    echo L$PARAM
          ;;
*)        if test $MUL = TRUE
          then
```

```
                echo  "MULT"
                echo  ";           Multiply routine sits in here"
                echo  ";           to multiply HL by DE and"
                echo  ";           return the result in HL."
                echo  "            RET"
                echo  ";"
        fi
        if test $DIV = TRUE
        then
                echo  "DIVN"
                echo  ";           Division routine sits in here"
                echo  ";           to divide HL by DE and"
                echo  ";           return the result in HL."
                echo  "            RET"
                echo  ";"
        fi
        if test $PRT = TRUE
        then
                echo  "PRINT"
                echo  ";           Print routine sits in here"
                echo  ";           to take the contents of HL"
                echo  ";           convert it from binary to"
                echo  ";           ASCII and print the chars."
                echo  "            RET"
                echo  ";"
        fi
        if test $TST = TRUE
        then
                echo  "TEST"
                echo  ";           Test routine sits in here."
                echo  ";           DE is compared with HL. The"
                echo  ";           accumulator contains a value"
                echo  ";           that says which test to do:"
                echo  ";              0  =    1  <>   2  <="
                echo  ";              3  >=   4  <    5  >"
                echo  ";           HL is set to 1 if condition"
                echo  ";           is true and 0 if false."
                echo  "            RET"
                echo  ";"
        fi
        ;;
    esac
done
```

Assuming that you call this program by the name '**trans**' then it can be used as follows:

$ **bcom** <**test.bas** | **trans** > **test.asm**

This command line uses the compiler from Chapter 16 to compile the TINY BASIC source program in the file **test.bas**. The ideal machine code output from the compiler is then piped into the translator for conversion to Z80 assembly code. The assembly code output is finally redirected into the file **test.asm**.

One last thing to remember is that you need to make the translator executable before you can use it as follows:

$ **chmod 700 trans**

A listing of **test.asm** produced by the previous translator run is:

```
;
; label 10
L10
;
; getnm 10
          LD         HL,10
;
; store a
          LD         (va),HL
;
; label 20
L20
;
; getnm 20
          LD         HL,20
;
; store b
          LD         (vb),HL
;
; label 30
L30
;
; getnm 30
          LD         HL,30
;
; store c
          LD         (vc),HL
;
; label 40
L40
;
; fetch a
          LD         HL,(va)
;
; fetch b
          PUSH       HL
          LD         HL,(vb)
;
; mult
          POP        DE
          CALL       MULT
;
; getnm 12
          PUSH       HL
          LD         HL,12
;
; fetch c
          PUSH       HL
          LD         HL,(vc)
;
; mult
          POP        DE
          CALL       MULT
;
; tstge
          POP        DE
          LD         A,3
          CALL       TEST
```

```
;
; jump 80
        LD      A,H
        OR      L
        JP      NZ,L80
;
; label 50
L50
;
; fetch a
        LD      HL,(va)
;
; minus
        LD      A,H
        CPL
        LD      H,A
        LD      A,L
        CPL
        LD      L,A
        INC     HL
;
; getnm 5
        PUSH    HL
        LD      HL,5
;
; subn
        EX      DE,HL
        POP     HL
        OR      A
        SBC     HL,DE
;
; print
        CALL    PRINT
;
; label 60
L60
;
; fetch a
        LD      HL,(va)
;
; getnm 1
        PUSH    HL
        LD      HL,1
;
; addn
        POP     DE
        ADD     HL,DE
;
; store a
        LD      (va),HL
;
; label 70
L70
;
; goto 40
        JP      L40
;
; label 80
L80
;
; fetch a
        LD      HL,(va)
;
```

```
; fetch a
        PUSH    HL
        LD      HL,(va)
;
; mult
        POP     DE
        CALL    MULT
;
; print
        CALL    PRINT
;
; label 90
L90
;
; stop
        HALT
;
;
MULT
;       Multiply routine sits in here
;       to multiply HL by DE and
;       return the result in HL.
        RET
;
PRINT
;       Print routine sits in here
;       to take the contents of HL
;       convert it from binary to
;       ASCII and print the chars.
        RET
;
TEST
;       Test routine sits in here.
;       DE is compared with HL. The
;       accumulator contains a value
;       that says which test to do:
;          0  =    1  <>    2  <=
;          3  >=   4  <     5  >
;       HL is set to 1 if condition
;       is true and 0 if false.
        RET
;
```

Suggested further reading

It is always very difficult when looking at a large collection of related books on the shelves in a bookshop to know which ones are going to be the most readable and the best value for money. Bearing the cost of computing books in mind, I have searched my shelves and have compiled the following list of my favourites, all of which follow on from some topic introduced in this volume. The suggestions are presented in no particular order, but the ones with an asterisk (*) by the title are especially worth a read:

* *The UNIX System V Environment*, S.R. Bourne, 1982, Addison-Wesley. Good general purpose UNIX reference book.

The UNIX C-shell Field Guide, G. Anderson and P. Anderson, 1986, Prentice-Hall. Covers the other major shell available on most UNIX systems. The C-shell is a better shell for interactive work than the Bourne shell you have seen, but not as good for the programming work you have done. And it is particularly the programming aspects I wanted to deal with.

UNIX Text Processing, D. Dougherty and T. O'Reilly, 1987, Hayden Books. Text processing using UNIX tools like **troff** and **nroff** is another subject I have not covered here. This is because programming does not require text editing facilities beyond those you have seen in **ed** and **vi**, consequently most students do not go any further in this area.

Advanced Programmers' Guide to UNIX System V, R. Thomas, L.R. Rogers and J.L. Yates, 1985, McGraw-Hill. Good book on creating your own software tools using both C and the Bourne and C shells.

UNIX for Super Users, E. Foxley, 1985, Addison-Wesley. This is a good look at UNIX from the system administrator's point of view rather than that of an ordinary user.

The Design of the UNIX Operating System, M.J. Bach, 1986, Prentice-Hall. Fairly detailed look at some of the UNIX internal algorithms. Not a book for the complete beginner but readable all the same.

Operating Systems: design and implementation, A.S. Tanenbaum, 1987, Prentice Hall. Particularly good book on operating system design principles with special reference to MINIX, a very close UNIX look-alike operating system. The source code for MINIX (written in 'C') is presented in the book along with full details of its operation.

UNIX Systems for Microcomputers, R. Burgess, Blackwell Scientific Publications. This is a book about putting UNIX to work within a system. It also contains a readable discussion on UNIX standards and the direction in which UNIX is evolving.

The C Programming Language, B.W. Kernighan and D.M. Ritchie, 1988, Prentice-Hall. The standard 'C' reference book by the authors of the language itself. Quite expensive but still the best reference book, in my opinion.

The Small-C Handbook, J.E. Hendrix, 1984, Prentice-Hall (Brady Books). Details the design and implementation (including listings in 'C') of a small-C compiler.

Debugging C, R. Ward, 1986, Que Corporation. Outlines many of the problems you have seen, but it also attempts to provide techniques and software listings to help overcome some of them.

The C++ Programming Language, B. Stroustrup, 1986, Addison-Wesley. Details what is claimed to be the next development in the evolution of C — only time will tell.

How to Solve it by Computer, R.G. Dromey, 1982, Prentice-Hall. Very good presentation of different data structures and algorithms for their manipulation.

Software: design, implementation and support, D.J. Leigh, D. Hatter and R.W. Newton, 1987, Paradigm. Contains some good information about software design and the professional approach to its implementation and support.

Writing Interactive Compilers and Interpreters, P.J. Brown, 1979, John Wiley and Sons. Very good and readable introduction to the subject with most of the examples based around the construction of a BASIC interpreter. Well worth reading.

Recursive Descent Compiling, A.J.T. Davis and R.Morrison, 1981, Ellis Horwood. Good book on recursive descent for those who want more detail than has been given here.

Exercises

CHAPTER 1

Q1

What is the kill character on your system and what is it used for?

A1

The character is system-dependent but is probably an at (@) symbol. This character is used to delete a whole line of input that you are typing, if you spot errors in the line before you press return.

Q2

What information is provided by the command **stty −a**?

A2

The **stty** command is used to examine and set the operating characteristics of your terminal. When followed by the −a parameter the **stty** command will display all of the terminal option values and settings currently in use. Many of the settings displayed may not mean too much to you at present, but the first line of the display should be fairly obvious as it contains the current values for such things as the kill, quit, erase and interrupt characters.

Q3

What key sequences correspond to the xoff and xon characters, and what do they do?

A3

The xoff and xon characters provide a simple mechanism that allows you to stop and start the flow of characters to your terminal. The xoff character is generated at the keyboard by pressing the 'control' and 's' keys together (ctrl–s). This will stop the computer from sending characters. The xon character is generated by pressing the 'control' and 'q' keys together (ctrl–q) and will allow the computer to resume sending characters to your terminal.

Q4

What types of files are kept in the directory **/etc**?

A4

The directory **/etc** contains mainly files and commands that deal with the administration of the system. These include things like the system password file (**/etc/passwd**) and the message of the day file (**/etc/motd**) that you get to see when you logon to the system. These files are mainly updated by the system administrator and you should certainly find that you do not have enough system privilege to change them.

Q5

Construct a list of the special keyboard key sequences available on your system with notes for their use. For reference purposes you might like to pencil them into the table below:

Key sequence	Notes

CHAPTER 2

Q1

If you are working on a terminal session and you do not want to be interrupted by other users on the system, what command should you give to prevent them from contacting you with **write**?

A1

You should give the command:

    mesg n

This will deny other users write access permission to your terminal (something that they do have by default).

Q2

If you issue the command from the answer to Q1, will that also prevent other users from sending you **mail** on the system?

A2

This is something that you can only really find out by trying it, and you should always be prepared to try out little experiments in order to find out things like this about your system. In fact, messages sent to you via **mail** are stored in a personal mail file that is associated with your login name. As the **mesg n** command only affects other users trying to access your terminal directly it will not prevent them sending you mail.

Q3

How would you find out if any of the users on your system have not chosen a password for themselves?

A3

As you know, all the system password information related to each user login name is stored in the system file **/etc/passwd**. The second field on each line of that file (i.e. between the first and second colon) contains a user's password in encrypted form. If you find a line on which the second field is empty then that user would not need to supply a password when logging on. Finding a line like:

    fred::400:400:fred smith:/usr/fred:/bin/sh

would mean that anyone would be able to logon as Fred Smith just by giving the name **fred** in return to the login: prompt. In this situation the system would not ask for a password but would log you straight in using **/usr/fred** as your home directory and giving you all the access permissions of the real Fred Smith. Seeing how easy it is to login as anyone who has not chosen a password, you can see that if you are in this position then it is important to choose a password as soon as possible, and to keep it secret.

Q4

Work out a command line that will change your current working directory to
/usr/bin but using only a relative path name.

A4

Remember that a relative path name is one that does not start with a slash (**/**)
character. This means that it is specified relative to your current directory
rather than the root directory. In order to specify how to get to somewhere
from your current position you need to know where your current position
actually is. You can get this information with the **pwd** command. Suppose
that **pwd** returns the value **/usr/you** meaning your home directory, then
the situation is as follows:

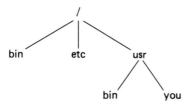

As you can see, **/usr/you** and **/usr/bin** both share **/usr** as a common
parent. To get from one to the other then you just need to go up to **/usr** and
down the other side. This can be done with the command:

    $ cd . ./bin

Q5

Create a directory structure within your home directory that corresponds to
the following directory map:

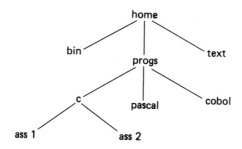

A5

One possible sequence of commands to generate this tree would be:

```
$ cd
$ mkdir bin progs text
$ cd progs
$ mkdir c pascal cobol
$ cd c
$ mkdir ass1 ass2
```

Q6

Using the directory structure from Q5 work out both an absolute and relative path so that a program running in the directory **ass1** can access a file called **data** in the directory **text**.

A6

There is enough information on the Q5 diagram to work out a relative path name from **ass1** to the file data in the **text** directory. To start with you need to go up three levels from **ass1** through **c** and **progs** to **home** and then down again into **text** finally accessing the file **data** as follows:

. . / . . / . ./text/data

In order to work out an absolute path to **data** from the root directory (/) you need to know the absolute path to your home directory. If I assume again that this is **/usr/you** then the absolute path to **data** becomes:

/usr/you/text/data

CHAPTER 3

Q1

What will be the output from the following simple commands:

ls −1 *
PS1 = UNIX:
cat /etc/passwd | wc −1

A1

if the **ls** command is given the name of a file as a parameter then using the −1 option as well, will list the long-form of the information about that file. If **ls −1** is given the name of a directory as a parameter then you will get a long listing of the information about all the files in that directory. When an asterisk (*) is used as a parameter, **ls** gets presented with all the items in the current directory, ordinary files and subdirectories and will consequently give a long listing of the lot. From within certain large directories this listing may extend to several screenfuls of file information. Piping the output from **ls −1 *** into more allows you to see the output from **ls** one screenful at a time.

The second command simply assigns the value 'UNIX:' to the standard shell variable **PS1** and as such does not really produce any output. However, you will notice that after entering this line your prompt has changed from $ to UNIX:.

The third command line is similar to some other examples you have seen where the output from a command is piped into **wc −l** to count how many lines of output the command gives. Piping the output from **cat/etc/passwd** into **wc −l** will just count the number of lines in the system password file. But remember that each user login requires one line of that file so that what the command line does in fact is to count the number of login names to your system.

Q2

Write down the complete sequence of commands you would need to enter during a terminal session to produce and run a shell script which will create two extra copies of a file whose name is given as a parameter to the shell script. The names of the extra files should be the same as the name of the original file but with the letters 'a' or 'b' appended to the end.

A2

The shell script itself will just contain two **cp** commands with suitable parameters to make the two file copies. The text of the shell script can be entered into a file using **cat**. After creation the shell script will need to be made executable with **chmod** and can then be run. A sample terminal session to do these things might be:

```
$ cat > newfiles
cp $1 $1a
cp $1 $1b
< ctrl-d >
$ newfiles filename
$ ls
filename filenamea filenameb newfiles
```

Q3

Execute the following command sequence:

```
$ sh
$ ps
$
```

Use the information from the **ps** output to draw a diagram similar in style to Figs 3.1 and 3.2 showing what processes you have running for you and what state each is in.

A3

When the sequence starts you have a shell running that gives you your $

prompt. Executing the command **sh** causes a child process (**sh**) to be forked and executed and the parent shell to wait (**sleep**). The running child (**sh**) command is in fact another copy of the shell and it is this second (child) shell that now gives you a prompt while the parent shell sleeps. You can see this better if you use **PS1** to change the parent shell prompt before you start. Giving the second shell the **ps** command causes it to fork and **exec ps** and then the second shell itself sleeps. This is the information that you get from **ps** — that there are two shells and the **ps** command running. When **ps** ends you will get a prompt back but it will come from the second shell not the first:

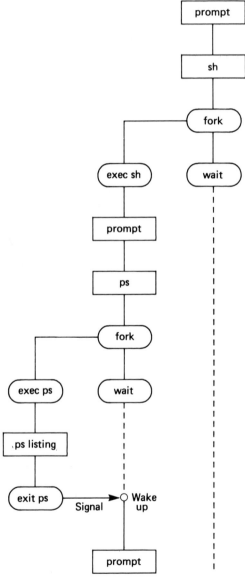

Before you can get a prompt back from the first shell you will need to terminate its child (the second shell) so that a signal will be sent to wake it up. As you know the way to terminate a shell is to use the exit command or the EOF (ctrl–d) sequence.

CHAPTER 4

Q1

Give **ed** command lines to perform the following actions:

(a) Find the number of lines in the text;
(b) Find the number of the current line;
(c) Print out the previous line of text;
(d) Replace 'and' by '&' in the current line;
(e) Delete this line and the following two;
(f) Delete part of the current line from 'aa' to 'zz';
(g) Delete everything after 'end' from the current line;
(h) Delete the first six lines of the file;
(i) Find the next three or more digit number;
(j) Find the first previous line containing a capital letter;
(k) Add the contents of file 'next' to the end of this one;
(l) Find the previous occurrence of '9.9';
(m) Insert text beyond end of file.

A1

(a) =
(b) .=
(c) .−1p
(d) s/and/1\&/gp
(e) .,.+2d
(f) s/aa.*zz//p
(g) s/end.*/end/p
(h) 1,6d
(i) /[0−9][0−9][0−9]/p
(j) ?[A−Z]?p
(k) r next
(l) ?9\.9?p
(m) $a

CHAPTER 5

Q1

Write a shell script that will search a file for lines containing the word UNIX, translate all upper-case letters in these lines to lower case and sort the resulting lines of text into descending alphabetical order.

A1

This problem needs three of the UNIX tools to sort it out, all bolted together into a single pipeline as follows:

```
$ cat > search
grep UNIX $1 | tr [A–Z] [a–z] | sort –r
< ctrl–d >
$ chmod 700 search
$
```

Q2

Write command lines to read the contents of a specified input file and perform the following actions:

(a) Delete the first 10 lines of the file;
(b) Print only lines containing at least one capital letter;
(c) Sort the input lines then replace 'NSP' by 'SP' and print the result;
(d) Do the same as part (c) but perform the sort last — what is the difference?

A2

(a) sed 1,10d filename
(b) sed –n /[A–Z]/p filename
(c) sort filename | sed s/NSP/SP/
(d) sed s/NSP/SP/ filename | sort

Part (c) and part (d) can produce different results. Part (c) sorts lines containing NSP while part (d) sorts lines containing SP.

CHAPTER 6

Q1

Write shell scripts to perform each of the following functions:

(a) Check the passwords file to see if a given login name exists. Give a suitable message and exit value;
(b) Check the directory flag and owner permission bits for a given file and

produce a report giving the values of these bits;

(c) Give a shell-like prompt and take command lines but only allow the user access to a restricted set of commands;

(d) Same as (b) but the program should accept multiple file names on the command line and ambiguous file names (using * and ?) as well.

A1

(a)
```
OP=/dev/null
if grep $1 /etc/passwd >$OP 2>$OP
then
    echo $1 is a valid login name
    exit 0
else
    echo $1 is NOT a valid login name
    exit 255
fi
```
(b)
```
FLAG=FALSE
echo"You can \c"
if test −r $1
then
    echo "read \c"
    FLAG=TRUE
fi
if test −w $1
then
    echo "write \c"
    FLAG=TRUE
fi
if test −d $1
then
    if test −x $1
    then
        echo "search \c"
        FLAG=TRUE
    fi
else
    if test −x $1
    then
        echo "execute \c"
    FLAG=TRUE
    fi
fi
if test $FLAG = FALSE
then
```

```
          echo "do nothing with \c"
    fi
    if test —d $1
    then
        echo the directory $1
    else
        echo the file $1
    fi
    exit 0
```

(c) ```
    while echo "> > \c" ; read CMD PARAM
    do
        case $CMD in
        1s)   ls $PARAM I grep —v rshell
              ;;
        ps)   ps $PARAM I grep —v rshell
              ;;
        *)   echo thats not allowed
              ;;
        esac
    done
```

Here the text should be stored in a file called 'rshell'. When run, **rshell** will give the prompt  > >  and wait for input. Notice that the only commands that will do any thing ae **ls** and **ps**, both of which have references to **rshell** removed from their output with **grep -v**. Any other command entered will give the message 'thats not allowed'.

(d)  ```
    for $i
    do
        # ANSWER TO PART (A) IN HERE
        # WITH REFERENCES TO $1 ALL
        # CHANGED TO $i
    done
```

CHAPTER 7

The best exercise for Chapter 7 is to try changing the layout of the sample programs to start to find a layout style to suit you and to convince yourself that changing style does not alter the meaning of your programs to the compiler.

Another good exercise is to introduce some errors into some of the programs to get a feel for the types of error messages that are produced by your compiler. This will help you to know what sorts of things to look for when error messages are given from compiling larger programs.

CHAPTER 8

Q1

Given that a=6, b=4, c=5 and d=3, what is the value of each of the following expressions:

(a) x = a > b
(b) (a == b) ? 0 : (a < b) ? −1 : 1
(c) c++ +d
(d) − −−c
(e) a ^b < < d
(f) b & d && a
(g) a ^d ^d
(h) c > > d | a
(i) a % c % a
(j) a | b ^b

A1

(a) 1
(b) 1
(c) 8
(d) −4
(e) 38
(f) 0
(g) 6
(h) 6
(i) 1
(j) 6

Q2

Use the following operand values 2, 3, 6 and 7 exactly once each, in each part (a–e) below. What you have to do is to generate expressions using these operands and any operators you like that will result in the following answer values:

(a) 41
(b) 6
(c) 13
(d) 19
(e) 1

A2

Possible answers are:

(a) (6 + 7) * 3 + 2
(b) (6 && 7) + 2 + 3
(c) (3 > > 2) + 6 + 7
(d) (6 ^3) + 2 * 7
(e) (7 % 3) + (6 % 2)

Do not worry if your answers were different, there are many alternatives that are equally correct (and maybe simpler!)

CHAPTER 9

Q1

Modify the lower-case to upper-case translation program so that it will translate the upper-case letters A–J into the digits 0–9.

A1

The simplest way is just to alter the first two **#define** statements as follows:

```
#define LITTLEA 'A'
#define BIGA '0'
```

This solution is not the best as the **#defines** are no longer meaningful. It would be better to use:

```
#define BIGA 'A'
#define ZERO '0'
```

and then change LITTLEA for BIGA and BIGA for ZERO throughout the program.

Q2

Modify the program again so that it translates upper-case letters A–Y into upper-case letters B–Z.

A2

After Q1 this is quite easy using the two **#defines**:

```
#define BIGA 'A'
#define BIGB 'B'
```

Q3

Having made the modification in Q2 will the program still work on the EBCDIC character code?

A3

No! As with the original program, to work with EBCDIC all the letters A–Y must be as far from the letters B–Z as A is from B. Unfortunately for EBCDIC this is not the case. However, the program still works for ASCII code.

CHAPTER 10

Q1

Write a program in 'C' to read in characters until EOF and output the ASCII codes for the characters as decimal numbers, printing the codes for 16 characters on each line separated by spaces.

A1

```
#include <stdio.h>
main()
{
   int c,count;
   count = 0;
   while ((c = getchar()) != EOF)
   }
     printf("%d ",c);
     count++;
     if (count % 16 == 0)
        printf("\n");
   }
   printf("\n");
}
```

Q2

Modify the 'Funny file listing' program so that it too prints 16 characters on a line.

A2

```
#include <stdio.h>
main()
{
    int c,count;
    count = 0;
    while ((c = getchar()) != EOF)
    {
        if (c < ' ' || c > '}')
            putchar('.');
        else
            putchar(c):
        count++;
        if (count % 16 == 0)
            putchar('\n');
    }
}
```

CHAPTER 11

Q1

Write a new version of the **strcpy()** routine given in this chapter that uses arrays rather than pointers:

A1

```
strcpy(a1,a2)
char a1[],a2[];
{
    int i;
    for (i = 0; a1[i] = a2[i]; i++);
}
```

Q2

Write a version of the UNIX command **echo** which just repeats its command line parameters to the screen.

A2

```
#include <stdio.h>
main(argc,argv)
int argc;
char *argv[];
{
    int i,j;
```

```
    for (i = 1: i < argc; i++)
    {
    for (j = 0; argv[i][j]; j++)
        putchar(argv[i][j]);
      putchar('');
    }
    putchar ('\n');
}
```

This is quite a tough question to answer — do not be too bothered if you could not sort it out, just make sure you understand my solution.

CHAPTER 12

Q1

Write a version of the UNIX **cat** command. Remember that it can take input from a set of files specified on the command line or from the standard input if no files are specified.

A1

```
#include <stdio.h>
main(argc,argv)
int argc;
char *argv[];
{
   FILE *fp,*fopen();
   if (argc == 1)
      cat(stdin);
      else
        for (i = 1; i < argc; i++)
        {
          fp = fopen(argv[i],"r");
          cat(fp);
          fclose(fp);
        }
}
cat(fptr)
FILE *fptr;
{
    int c;
    while ((c = getc(fptr)) != EOF)
        putchar(c);
}
```

Q2

Without referring back in the book, what output did the following set of **printf** statements produce?

```
printf("!%6d!\n", 123);
printf("!%-6d!\n",456);
printf("!%06d!\n",789);
printf("!%2x!\n",205);
printf("!%2X!\n",205);
printf("!%02x!\n",12);
printf("!%10.2e!\n",123.456);
printf("!%10.3E!\n",123.456);
printf("!%10s!\n","string");
printf("!%-10s!\n","string");
printf("!%10.4s!\n","string");
printf("!%1u!\n",12345L);
```

A2

OK ... look back and see!!

CHAPTER 13

Q1

Write two versions of a program that will separate out the 4 bytes in a 32-bit integer and print them in reverse order. Use a union in the first version to split the **int** up into its component bytes and any other method for the second version.

A1a

```
main()
{
    int j;
    union
    {
        int i;
        char c[4];
    } mix;
    mix.i = 0x12345678;
    for (j = 0; j < 4; j++)
        printf("%2x",mix.c[3-j]);
}
```

A1b

The other one I will leave for you to sort out!!

Index